Declutter your home
Make Money

How to Turn Your Old & Unwanted Stuff into Cash Fast!

By

Rebecca O'Brien

Copyrighted Material

Copyright © 2021 – **Parma Books**

All Rights Reserved.

No part of this publication may be reproduced, stored in a retrieval system or transmitted in any form or by any means, electronic, mechanical, photocopying, recording or otherwise without the proper written consent of the copyright holder, except as permitted under Sections 107 & 108 of the 1976 United States Copyright Act, without the prior written permission of the publisher.

Parma Books publishes its books and guides in a variety of electronic and print formats, Some content that appears in print may not be available in electronic format, and vice versa.

Cover & Book Design by Robin Albright

First Edition

Contents

Introduction 6

Chapter 1: Decluttering for Peace and Clarity 13

Chapter 2: Downsize for Sustainability..................................... 18

Chapter 3: Materialistic to minimalistic 22

Chapter 4: Reorganizing for efficiency 26

Chapter 5: Emergency Fund – Creating and Maintaining a Cash Stash 33

Chapter 6: Need Versus Want – Learning to Let it Go 37

Chapter 7: How to Let Go of Things By Disassociating Yourself From the Memory Associated With the Items 42

Chapter 8: How to Stop Emotional Shopping and Spending....... 48

Chapter 9: General Selling Need-to-Know 55

    Sell-almost-anything Sites.. 56

    Category-specific Sales Sites 65

Chapter 10: Items to Let Go: What Should I Sell?..................... 67

    Antiques 70

    Appliances 79

Art	84
Baby Gear	88
Books	96
CDs and DVDs	102
Clothing	107
Collectibles	122
Crafting Supplies	133
Décor	135
Electronics	141
Furniture	148
Gift Cards	152
Housewares	156
Jewelry	159
Kids' Stuff	173
Musical Instruments	178
Office	183
Outdoor and Gardening	187
Pet	190
School Supplies	193

Sports Gear and Memorabilia 195

Tools..208

Vehicles 212

Video Games 226

Vintage Items 234

Chapter 11: How to Throw a Great Garage Sale.......................*239*

Conclusion *243*

Introduction

Let's start with a moment of gratitude. A moment of thankfulness that we know a life that would allow us to have so many things that we are able to sell some or all of them and still be able to function in our daily lives. There are many who never have and never will know the feeling of having too much, a little extra, or even just enough.

Rant done. The reality is that many Americans have a lot of stuff. Sometimes some very cool stuff, but a lot of stuff, oftentimes unnecessary stuff. Stuff that can be decluttered, downsized, minimized, and organized to create an emergency cash fund. ClosetMaid conducted a survey of 2,000 Americans about the items they have in their home. Some interesting numbers were compiled:

Over half have over 20 miscellaneous and unnecessary items.

19% of people have so much extra stuff that they have been told by someone close that they are a hoarder.

15% of survey respondents said, "They would get rid of an item only to secretly keep and hide it."

48% said the excess clutter creates panic, stress, and anxiety.

Even though I live a simple, humble life, or because I do, I myself tend to collect things and hold onto them. I live in the country on a beautiful acre and a quarter of a mini forest. Nestled in this wooded little wonderland is a small RV that I inherited from my grandmother. It is filled with stuff. Inside of the RV, there are dishes, a couple small appliances, tons of clothes, art supplies, an electric drum set, Christmas decorations, and I don't even know what else. As I research and work on this text, I will be using these same methods to get my life decluttered, downsized, minimized, and organized to create a cash fund.

If I had that space at least decluttered, I could possibly use it as a home office, a space to film YouTube videos, a place to get away from whoever is in the main house with me, or maybe, just maybe even sell the RV itself once it was empty. The point is, I am going on this journey with you.

Being a simple, humble soul, I have a good amount of experience buying preowned items. I have found that even when I do have the money to get something brand new, it's hard for me to do. Not just because I hate to pay full price, but also because I also think about the impact of all of us continuing to buy new stuff has on the environment.

When you buy something that has been preowned, you reduce the amount of waste going into the environment and help to make sure that all items live their proper life and afford the universe their greatest value. So, you save money, purchase from someone which helps out their situation, help the environment, and develop another good, conscientious habit.

With that being said, a lot of my selling my stuff experience has been using good ole Craigslist, Facebook marketplace ad groups (my favorite at this point), g, yard/garage sales, flea markets, and community festivals. I have avoided other online options and apps because I did not want to have to deal with the fees and the shipping process. Rather, I would have chosen to electronically meet someone, make arrangements, meet in person, exchange the item and the currency, and part ways.

The research and time that goes into this text will include my personal experiences, lessons learned, and what I am learning new for myself and you. If I haven't personally done it, I will make sure to get as much info as I can. Everyone has different needs, lives, and therefore different stuff, so this text will attempt to cover it all. Along the way, I myself will be learning new things because, in today's climate, flexibility and ingenuity will be invaluable.

Today is a different scenario for many reasons. The biggest one being that we are living in the middle of a chapter of history. I have to acknowledge it because it has changed a lot of our operations, is continuing to change almost daily, and will continue to create a change that may be very long-lasting. This is the beginning of June 2020.

At this point in dealing with a global pandemic, over 40 million people unemployed, and now we are in the midst of a series of protests across the country. Another moment to be heard, one of condolences and respect to those who have suffered and are suffering still. My heart is with you.

All of these facts are important because they will affect the way you need to do things. A lot of people are suffering greatly and are also trying to sell their things. This will create a saturation in the market of private sellers and a reduction in the number of buyers. I have been working on selling some of my things and helping my mother do the same and am seeing the trend for myself.

So, those of us fortunate to, who may be so unfortunate as

to have to part with it now, use that stuff in your home to do whatever you want/ need to.

Pay a bill(s).

Fix the car.

Go to the doctor.

Get the A/C repaired.

Buy that pool for the kids, so they get off the electronics and outside.

Become a prepper of a different variety and invest in solar panels to change your energy source for the impending doom that is coming from the recession.

Get all the kids, new school clothes and shoes.

Rent a car and take a trip to Colorado.

Whatever you want to do – it's your stuff that you are

selling for whatever reason to do with as you please. And in the process of selling your stuff, your space and your spirit will become lighter. There is a good amount of work involved in several aspects, which will require labor, time, and sometimes investment. Then there's the emotional side: coming across an old picture, journal entry, or item; having to let go of a sentimental item; some experience grief of letting go; reliving an old memory from its attachment to the item. Everyone's experience is personal and unique to them and their situation.

Chapter 1: Decluttering for Peace and Clarity

The word clutter literally means disordered, scattered, crowded, and/or confused. For many people, those types of words can invoke feelings such as angst, anxiety, and chaos. So, by very definition, when you DE-clutter, you are doing the opposite. An environment free of clutter helps to create moods and spaces of order, peace, clarity, and purpose.

This is what the revolutionary, decluttering, professional

organizer guru Marie Kondo does. Before she published her book, *The Life-Changing Magic of Tidying Up,* in 2014, she was already a successful Japanese cleaning consultant whose goal was to help her clients find peace and balance by decluttering their living spaces. Her theory, the KonMari Method, follows the philosophy that you can eliminate all of the unnecessary stuff by determining whether or not each item brings a spark of joy and is therefore worthy of being kept.

When I first read that, I thought, well, there's no way that everything is going to bring me joy. How would that even work? I had to really think about that for a second. I can be both a very practical, logical, incredibly efficient person and, at the same time, a very emotional, spontaneous, hormonally driven fruit loop.

So, I looked at things with a different view. I found joy in my things, on both sides -both the sensibly and fancifully. For example, I have a tiny kitchen, and I use the only large kitchen cabinet to store all of my pots, pans, mixing bowls, and other large kitchenware. When I think of the kitchenware that is my favorite to use, there is a spark of joy when I think of the yumminess I can create. When I think of the extra items or how I am going to have to rearrange the whole cabinet of wares just to get to my favorite sauté pan, I feel frustrated and anxious. That was when the concept started to make more sense to me. I had to use that same thought process when it came to all of the items I was going to get rid of.

With the KonMari Method, there are six basic rules to adhere to:

1. Commit yourself to the decluttering journey. (And mean it)

I have been meaning to clean out my storage space for longer than I care to put in print. Saying it offhandedly is one thing; making a commitment and following through is another.

2. Envision the life/lifestyle you want.

I want a clean, healthy, happy, peaceful existence where there is continuous progress, healing, and restoration. I don't think semi-hoarding and not knowing where half my stuff is helps get me there.

3. Thank the item for serving its purpose before discarding it.

A perpetual attitude of thanksgiving is crucial for me. Even towards nature, animals, and even inanimate objects.

4. Declutter by category by category, not by the space it holds.

For example, clothing – there may be summer items in the closet and drawers now and the cooler weather pieces in a storage space elsewhere in the house. Gather them all together for one decluttering session.

5. Follow the steps in proper order.

The proper sequence ensures optimal results. If you're baking a cake, you can't frost it before it bakes.

6. Most importantly – find joy.

Not only will it help you with the decluttering process, but it will also help to solidify an attitude and mentality of happiness. Seeking and finding joy seems to be the real meaning of life.

Chapter 2: Downsize for Sustainability

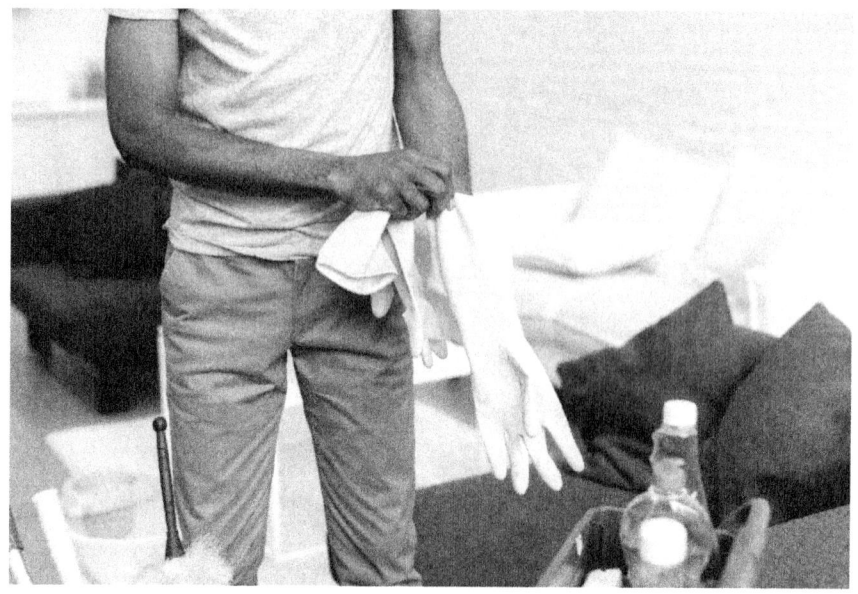

Downsizing means that, for whatever reason, you are moving from a larger living space to a smaller living space. In doing so, it becomes necessary to reduce the amount and size of the furniture, appliances, clothing, décor, and other miscellaneous items that take up space in the abode.

It doesn't always have to refer to the process of moving from one home to another. Sometimes it can refer to the downsizing of personal belongings, downsizing of maintenance, downsizing of stress. The reduction in volume is the whole point in the downsizing process.

There is an interesting concept out there that addresses the topic of letting go of material things to live a more organized, efficient, reduced stress lifestyle. It is called 'Swedish death cleaning' and is based on the premise that as one reaches middle age, they do not want to leave a giant pile of mess for their loved ones to sift through. In a sense, it can be considered the anti-Kondo-Mari method. This means that rather than going through your things with the intent of finding what sparks joy, you are on a mission to leave behind only what others will find joy in and reduce their stress.

For some, it can be a good idea to have a family member present during this process. It will be a good opportunity to talk about whatever wishes one may have for when their time comes, walk down memory lane together, and ease some of the burden and discomfort that come with realizing your own mortality.

It is also helpful to take this time to make sure that you

have some things in writing. Now, before you go thinking, 'well, I'm only 35 years old, why would I think that way'? Because tomorrow is promised to no one, that's why. Anyhow, take this time to write down passwords, login information, and any other paperwork or electronic documentation that someone would need access to if you were gone tomorrow.

Dive right in by going into the closets where clothes, shoes, bags, and other things can be easily non-emotionally sorted out before you tackle the sometimes-difficult things like photographs and mementos. As is in the purpose of this book, sort through and sell what you can, making sure to leave certain people with certain items and selling what is not sentimental.

Books are not always easy or profitable to sell, but you can give another reader joy when you donate your old reading material to places like churches, shelters, rehabilitation centers, hospitals, and other non-profit organizations.

The philosophy hinges on the fact that we do not need as many things as we tend to accumulate. Then, when we pass on, the laborious task of going through those items is then passed on to our loved ones. Being that they are already grieving, why add the burden of combing through all your clutter.

Although the theory is geared towards individuals coming closer to the end of their life, the idea is that anyone, at any age, can benefit from a decluttered, more organized life is universal.

While a lot of the Swedish death cleaning literature is focusing on people 65 or older, it really is a good philosophy that anyone can use to shed some of their excess materialism. I myself am 40 (almost 41) but am very aware of my mortality and have decided to give this thought process a serious try. There are definitely things that I can get rid of that I would not want my grown kids to stumble across. And in the process, I end up a few hundred pounds lighter in the extra stuff section, and hopefully at least a few hundred dollars heavier in the wallet area.

Chapter 3: Materialistic to minimalistic

Personally, I am all about live and let live. If you dig having lots of name brand things, have the funds to do so, and it brings you happiness – go for what you know.

If you personally believe in leading a lifestyle that subscribes to a minimalistic motto, that's cool too.

My question to either extreme – materialism or minimalism – if some sort of emergency/catastrophe occurred tomorrow, what items would you and your family need to survive and thrive?

Will the Gucci bag help feed the fam? Or would you have pared your belongings down to the point that you had no excess to draw on?

I think a careful middle ground is the best place to be. Living a sustainable life that does the least amount of harm to yourself, your family, people around you, and the environment seems like the most logical, fair way to be.

No matter what end of the socioeconomic scale you find yourself weighing in at, almost everyone in the United States can possibly have too much stuff. The idea of minimalism is not just to have as few belongings as possible. It is a constant lifestyle choice to focus on things other than things.

At this point in my blessedly beautiful life, I cannot brag about how much money I have; I don't have a brand-new car nor an amazing home with an inground pool in the backyard. I live simply but, to be honest, still on the excessive side when it comes to how much stuff I hold onto.

Minimizing could be massively helpful for me so that I can make better, more efficient use of the small space I have available. I mean, really, do I need a pan of every shape and size when I use the same 3 over and over again. In that same strain of thought, I have a massive amount of clothes. My weight tends to fluctuate, twenty pounds heavier than where I am now and twenty pounds lighter – depending on several factors.

A more minimalistic approach would be to only hold onto a few essential items from each set of sizes so that I don't have to buy new clothes but also so that I am not housing a small thrift store in the form of an RV in my yard either.

In reality, living a minimized life means minimizing excess stuff, excess stress, excess decisions, excess time going through said stuff, and reducing cost in a physical and monetary sense.

Going from a crowded, cluttered existence can also bring about a sort of grief from having to part ways with things that you placed so much value in. Once you do that, the items you will have left will hold an even greater value. For one, each item has to be special and useful for you to have decided to hold onto it. Then, because there are no backups or duplicates, each piece will be even more treasured.

Once committing to the minimized mindset, you will find yourself spending more time shopping but spending less money. This will come from realizing that frivolous expenditures dip into the possibility of extra savings and adding to the possibility of having too much stuff again. Therefore, each spending decision will be weighed more heavily.

Two big things that a minimalized lifestyle will help you achieve – the ability to do more with less and spend way less money. No more impulse buys and piles of things rarely used. Instead, everything you own will have a defined and clear purpose, allowing you to devote your time, money, resources, and energy to all the other things in life that matter besides things.

Chapter 4: Reorganizing for efficiency

"An organized home is a happy home," says the great Martha Stewart. When your space is well organized, it will be easier to keep your mind and life in order too.

The thought that having an organized house adds to overall increased efficiency is a simple thought process to follow. If you always know where everything is located, then there is never time wasted trying to locate your belongings when it's time to go, prepare a meal, get ready for bed, or any of the countless other tasks we perform in our homes on a regular basis.

There are many benefits to being organized and efficient. There is a decreased level in stress, an increase in the amount of and quality of sleep, more free time means more 'me' time, increased productivity at home and work, get more done in less time, gain a sense of control in your life and wellbeing, set a good example for kids or other people around you, project a better image of yourself to others, clear your head for other ventures, and you and the ability to gain energy and calm from the space around you.

Additionally, the ideal level of organization will mean that you have pared down the number of belongings in the dwelling to a level that allows you to have everything you need without being crowded with too much excess.

So, if your goal is to get organized and sell all of your excess stuff, organization will be key. How will you know what you have, what you have posted to sell, who is buying what, how much each item is worth and posted for if you are not thoroughly and completely organized?

When I embarked on the beginning of this journey, I have to admit that I not only had way too much stuff but that what I did have was completely disorganized. For a few years, I was a non-traditional student (I was over 25 years old), worked full time, and had family obligations. So, it also, unfortunately, meant that I tended to be on the go so much that if I couldn't find something, I simply bought another and went about my merry way.

By the time it came time to get myself and my space organized, I had duplicates of all kinds of items in all kinds of spaces and containers. I really didn't have the money to spend to buy those duplicates; it took up space I didn't have, added to my stress level when I could not locate something, and was overall a big mess.

Since I have been diligently working on becoming more organized, my work, study, and personal space are so much easier to use with no need to spend extra time looking for that pack of sticky notes, that favorite tee shirt, or a clean towel. I do believe that there are organizational possibilities for even the messiest, chaotic person.

24 tips for staying organized:

1) Use a picture ledge to hide cords and display your treasures at the same time

2) Use the walls to organize and save space. Hang individual canvas bins on even a hanging shoe organizer.

3) Use a kitchen cabinet door to create an organization station that houses passwords, coupons, keys, memos, etc., with a chalkboard vinyl.

4) Give everything a home. Then nothing will ever be out of place, and there will be a space for each item to return to.

5) Create an outbox area that is designated for things that need to leave, such as packages, mail, backpacks, store returns, etc., so they don't end up on the floor, kitchen table, or any other random spot.

6) Keep your daily routine in mind and put things where they work for you and your needs.

7) Use a tray on a coffee table or island. Let the tray catch all the small miscellaneous items – keys, remotes, loose change, etc.

8) Put a trash can in every room. That way, there is less to pile up or set to the side.

9) Create and keep a cleaning routine to keep everything fresh and in its place.

10) Let go of things you don't wear. Let go of the pile of socks to make that Pinterest sock rug, the old sweater that you won't wear outside of the front door – those types of things.

11) Cleaning supplies in a caddy. Makes it easier to tote from room to room when cleaning, and the supplies always have a home.

12) Empower the kids to organize themselves. Give them an alarm clock and a morning checklist of things that need to be done. Time management skills early on!

13) Put decorative shoe boxes/storage containers

around the house. Goes back to the theory of everything having a home.

14) Label storage boxes to avoid making a mess and wasting time digging through the wrong boxes.

15) Donate cookbooks. Keep your favorite recipes by making a copy and putting them in plastic sheet protectors inside a binder.

16) Say no to the round containers. They never make the most of the space inside of the square cabinets.

17) Say yes to lists. Keeping and using checklists will make it easier to stay organized ahead of time.

18) Plan ahead and always have a backup of everything – keys, deodorant, hair ties, anything that is essential and can be misplaced.

19) Put your important info in one place so that you can grab it in the case of an emergency.

20) Invest in good closet organization; it will be worth the time and money.

21) Separate seasonal clothes. It's so hard to dig through ten sweaters to find one tank top.

22) Use stacking bins. This is especially helpful when there is limited closet and drawer space.

23) Shower curtain rings make a great accessory ladder. Loop one to the top of a hanger and then attach more to organize scarves and belts.

24) Use a peg board for storage. Paint it to your liking, and then use this space for extra wall storage.

Chapter 5: Emergency Fund – Creating and Maintaining a Cash Stash

Different people will have different definitions of what constitutes an emergency and, of course, will have varying levels of abilities to handle the unexpected.

Many people are feeling the effects of not having an emergency fund set up right now, today. The pandemic of 2020 and the ensuing consequences have put over 30 million Americans out of work, some for close to three months now with no real sign of when things will go back to 'normal.'

When almost 80 percent of the American population lives paycheck to paycheck, the loss of three months of pay is devastating. Even if there was an emergency fund in place at the beginning of the pandemic, consequently, it may be long gone now.

Selling your stuff may not have been something even remotely contemplated as an option before the crisis hit. For many, it is no longer an option but a necessity. If you are one of those people, my heart goes out to you, and I hope that there is information in this text that helps you.

With all of that being said, it is especially important in today's political, social, economic, and health climate to make sure that you have a stash of funds and resources. What that number should look like is very situation-specific. It depends on where you live, what your situation is like there, how many people depend on you, what your monthly expenses are like if you or anyone else has any medical conditions, etc. The list is long and varied like people are.

Overall, most experts suggest that a proper emergency fund should be enough for three to six months of expenses. As stated previously, the U.S. and the whole world are dealing with a pandemic, and America specifically is also going through a civil rights crisis and the ensuing protests that have turned violent in many cases.

With that being said, even though the 'experts' have previously stated that three to six months is the average ideal emergency fund, I would think that it is probably much wiser to shoot for somewhere closer to a year. For some people, a year's worth of funds is always kept tucked into an account. For the rest of us, a year is an almost impossibly imaginable number.

To put the situation into perspective, there are many people who lost their jobs in middle February, early March and are still not working all the way through to now here in June, five months later. Many of those people are still not working. While the government has implemented helpful measures such as increased unemployment funds, increased access to programs such as food stamps, and the stimulus check that most

Americans received, it is still not enough.

2020 has made me realize now more than ever how crucial it is to create and maintain an emergency fund. I have personally been a dichotomy when it comes to money and preparedness. On one hand, I have a prepper-like mentality when it comes to expecting the best but being prepared for the worst. On the other hand, I also have the flakiness of a free spirit who isn't scared to leave a situation behind and go bartend and freelance until I'm ready to settle down again.

That's not going to work anymore. Since the pandemic started having such terrible consequences, my mindset is all about getting prepared and staying that way. Gone are the days of being able to live loose and fancy-free. Now is the time to stay in a mindset of being ready in case of the worst and ready to take care of myself and whoever else I may need to help.

Chapter 6: Need Versus Want – Learning to Let it Go

Another moment of gratitude is in order. There are many people around the world who do not even have what they need, let alone the luxury of having excess. There are too many people in the world that have had to go hungry, watch their baby cry with hunger, use dirty water to prepare food, and all other kinds of atrocities that most Americans will never know.

Even though I grew up very simply, I did not know hunger. All of my basic needs were always met. I didn't really start to want anything until I became a teenager and realized I was a lot different than a lot of the people around me, and I wanted the things necessary to be more like them. The reason I include that unsolicited piece of personal information is because my want was created by an emotional need to be accepted, not driven by a materialistic desire.

This, in turn, brings us to the point that there is more than one kind of need and many kinds of want. When a person has a physiological need that has to be met, they will experience a state of tension and stress, which will drive their behavior to reach the goal of meeting that need. It goes like this:

The strength of the need corresponds to the levels of tension and stress. The stronger the need, the stronger the tension and stress.

Once the intensity of the tension reaches a certain point, it becomes unpleasant and uncomfortable.

If the need is not met, and the tension continues, the person will engage in activity to meet the goal of meeting the need.

Once the goal is met, the tension is discharged.

So, what do we need?

There are three kinds of needs: organic, emotional, and economical. Organic needs are the basic human needs for survival. Air, water, food, habitable temperatures, shelter, rest, health – the things that you absolutely cannot live without. Emotional needs are affection, belongingness, security, achievement, intimacy. Economic needs are met by a suitable occupation that allows one to earn a living, spend their money according to need and desire, and reach goals such as purchasing land, homes, vehicles. You have to survive first before you are able to thrive.

Humans want what they need first, and once their basic needs are met, they want more; they want better. There is nothing wrong with wanting more. The desire to do better, be better, have more, be a better example is a great motivator to enact change from within. Maslow's hierarchy of needs tells us that a person cannot realize actualization of themselves until all of their needs, and most of their wants are met.

When thinking of how to distinguish between need and want, it's ok to say I want more than to just survive; I want to thrive. But when the want is all for material items, and it causes problems, then the time comes to analyze the why behind the want and redirect it. When a person finds themselves wanting nothing but material items, maybe it's time to look at what other wants need to be met.

At the most basic level, you want to live; you want to get past survival into a level of peace and comfort. You want to have economic security, social love, and acceptance, want to have a comfortable space to live, the desire for stimulation, and you want to live a life of freedom and liberty.

That doesn't sound like too much to ask for, does it? Life, liberty, and the pursuit of happiness are what most of us want. There are certain essential needs that have to be met in order to get to the wanted part of life.

Once the necessities are out of the way, and it comes time for the wants to take over, make sure that the wants are all in line with your ultimate goals. Will the new designer bag help you save for a down payment for a home? Does buying new scrapbooking supplies help you fix the air conditioner on the car? Will buying the newest kitchen appliance get the teenager in your life into the braces they need?

The bottom line is to make sure that all of your wants are motivators that are going to help you reach your goals and enhance your life, not add any more stress.

Chapter 7: How to Let Go of Things By Disassociating Yourself From the Memory Associated With the Items

Memory is a powerful thing. Without memories and the ability to remember, we would not be able to function in life. We remember things all day, every day. You must remember to take your medicine, put gas in the car, call to schedule appointments, finish assignments, pick something up from the store.

But what about the memories that stir emotions and take us back to a place, a moment in time. There are many common day occurrences that can evoke a memory. A song, a smell, an article of clothing, a personal belonging, food, there are so many triggers to bring about emotions and memories.

For many of us, memories associated with items may be the reason that we hold on to certain items in our homes. Don't feel bad about having all that extra stuff; you can't help it. Ever since you were a child, you have been gathering things to call your own, sometimes holding onto some things since infancy.

An article in *The British Psychological Society*, "The psychology of stuff and things" by Christian Jarrett, delves into the phenomena of needing, wanting, and having too much stuff.

In his text, he explores the fact that material possession starts in infancy when toddlers develop an "intense relationship with a specific 'attachment object'" (such as a blanket or toy). In a scientific study, researchers tested this concept by offering the children a duplicate of the object, a copy. Most of the children agreed and then reacted in horror when the researcher followed through and offered them an alternate object. The scientists tied this behavior to adulthood with this statement, "It's as if the children believed their special object had a unique essence, a form of magical thinking that re-appears in adulthood in our treatment of heirlooms … memorabilia and artwork".

The trend continues into adolescence, when material possessions become the most important when self-esteem is at its lowest in most human development. Even as our sense of self continues to grow and evolve, we still tend to use objects and items to define who we are. It seems that even as we mature, we continue to place importance on material possessions. This statement from the article sums up the final stage we find ourselves in as adults, "our things embody our sense of self-hood and identity still further, becoming external receptacles for our memories, relationships, and travels."

This integration of things, memories, and the importance we place on that combination is oftentimes the reason we end up with so many miscellaneous items. Marie Kondo asked if the item sparked joy. Magnusson, the 'Swedish death cleaning' guru, advised to clean up and let go before it's time to pass.

No one is saying to let go of treasure memories associated with items, especially from people who are no longer here. Instead, maybe there are ways to honor that person and those memories without holding onto too many things.

Tips on how to release your attachment to SO many things:

Start with something easy. Tackle an area or space that has things you can let go of easier to start a sense of accomplishment – an overfull mismatched sock drawer, an old pair of shoes that just never fit right: let them go.

Create time limitations. Don't let yourself get stuck in a time and memory portal. Give yourself a time limit and stick to it. Keeping an eye on the clock and the self-imposed limitation will help reduce the amount of time spent in memory lane.

Challenge yourself. In addition to placing a time limitation, set a goal for yourself. In the garage, if there are 10 boxes housing various items and memorabilia, make it a point to take it down to 6 or whatever number you feel comfortable with.

Essential or beautiful things only. Only keep what is essential and purposeful or those things that are beautiful. Beauty does not have to mean expensive, simply that you find it so. The less extraneous things that are surrounding your remaining essential and beautiful items, the more likely you are to really appreciate them.

Enlist some help or even just company. Some prefer to tackle everything solo, and that's ok. But a little support goes a long way when you need to be held accountable and maybe need a shoulder to cry on or a friendly face to laugh with to make the task easier.

Don't deny your emotions. Go ahead and connect with those thoughts and feelings. Explore the reason you're hanging onto that item. What does the item represent for you? Give yourself an opportunity to look at the memories you created and attached to the items. Then, thank the item for serving its purpose and helping you revisit those memories.

Without going into too much detail, I can say that there was a time in my life that I was quite the gypsy and did not hold onto things the way that I was supposed to. Once I settled down, I realized that I very much regretted not having certain items to pick up and walk down memory lane. In my journeys, I had lost pictures, mementos, memorabilia, and sometimes the only way to relive a moment is to have a little piece of the original experience.

However, you don't want to have so many little pieces of your past lying around that you are not fully able to live this life to your fullest. Some of the hardest things that I have the hardest time parting with are things that came from my kids or from people who are not here anymore.

Chapter 8: How to Stop Emotional Shopping and Spending

For the most part, we all do something to soothe ourselves, block out reality for a brief chunk of time, or just to cope with whatever is going on at the moment. Whatever method we choose, there are oftentimes consequences if it is not done in moderation. Whether you choose to ease your woes with food, alcohol, sex, shopping, gambling – there is a potential to overdo it and must suffer some consequences.

In this text, the focus will be on emotional shopping and spending. To be able to participate in the act of emotional shopping and spending, there must be the monies available to do us, whether it is with actual cash or on credit that will be due at an inflated rate.

People's relationship with wealth, money, possessions, and happiness is studied in the book, *The Psychological Science of Money* by Erik. Through extensive research, the author details the ways that money transforms from the necessary and primary way that we can meet our needs to the driving force behind almost every action we undertake throughout our lives.

In the book, Bijleveld highlights the correlation between money and happiness. "An abundance of research over many decades shows that although there is most definitely a positive relationship between wealth ... and happiness, it is typically quite modest and suffers considerably from diminishing returns".

Basically, he is saying that people who have plenty of money do not see money and possessions as being able to bring them happiness and that science and research support this. This statement also means that people of lower-income levels find a higher level of hedonic pleasure when they spend money on splurging rather than survival.

As is the case with any other vice, addiction, or bad habit, there are always signs that the continued act is becoming unhealthy and needs to be addressed.

Some signs that you are emotional spending:

Instant gratification drives your purchases – Don't feel bad. It's the same reason some people eat that extra portion of yumminess, the gambler places that extra bet, the drinker orders another shot. No one is better or worse than another but just an issue that needs some attention.

Escaping from reality – Taking time to find a special gift for someone is much different than regularly spending hours shopping, whether online or in person.

Spending to stay competitive – Only you know if the look you're rockin' made you have to take out yet another credit card. At the end of the day, living beyond your means, especially when doing so to keep up with others, will catch up to you.

Lots of makeovers – Shopping to upgrade, redesign, or fix what you don't love about yourself on the outside will never fix what's going on in your mind and heart.

Frequent shopper and returner – So... maybe you justify the shopping by saying that you return most of it anyway. You may want to examine why you are spending so much time on that entire process rather than some other fulfilling, productive activity.

Shopping is how you celebrate yourself – Love yourself, absolutely. Celebrate your beautifully designed, amazing self. But if that is the only way that you are treating yourself, or you are spending money you can't afford, you may want to reexamine the reasoning behind why and connect with yourself (as cheesy as that sounds).

Spending money when you're stressed about money – It feels strange to read it in print, but the fact is that many of us do it. When we feel uncertain about the future financially, there can be a tendency to overspend and overextend just in case another opportunity does not present itself, sort of a form of self-preservation.

Oftentimes, the first step to solving a problem is identifying that a problem exists at all. It can be an especially hard pill to swallow when you have suffered negative consequences from it and know that it could have been avoided. Don't wallow in that. Recognizing that there is a problem is the first hurdle to overcome.

How to STOP emotional shopping and spending:

Give yourself a break and then check yourself – Don't beat yourself up too much about it. Confront the emotions behind the actions so you can break the cycle. Then do what you can to break the cycle.

Identify triggers – Once you are aware of what you are doing, it will become easier to identify the internal and external forces that lead you to the negative behaviors. Holidays, anniversaries of events, birthdays, death dates, are all specific times that you know can set off emotional responses.

Unsubscribe and uninstall – Take your name off emails, physical mail, and apps that will send you messages, letters, and notifications. The temptation never seen is the temptation unknown.

Budget your treats – Set a limit on your unnecessary purchases. That way, you can still treat yourself without over splurging.

Use cash – Leaving your credit card at home and using only cash will help you to actually see and feel the exact amount of money you are spending, and you will be literally limited to the cash that you have on hand.

Stop autosaving credit card information – Marketing and website engineers are geniuses and make it so easy for you to store your credit card information. That way, it is one easy click to spend that money. If your information is not autosaved, you will have to think lo0nger about what you are buying.

Ask for help – Tell someone, or multiple people, that you are on this path of self-improvement. Having another person to be accountable to can be helpful.

Stick with the original intention – Ever find yourself with way more in the cart, whether virtually or in-person, than you started off shopping for? Well, before you complete that checkout, remove everything that was not on the original list/thought process, and only get what you went in for.

Alternate activities and interest – Replace the time you spend shopping with some other activity or interest; exercise and sunshine help to release feel-good hormones that offer similar rewards to the satisfaction of shopping.

Twenty-four-hour rule – Emotional shopping and spending are often impulsive. Give yourself an entire day, a whole twenty-four hours, before completing the transaction.

Chapter 9: General Selling Need-to-Know

In this next chapter, we'll talk about general advice and stuff that I sincerely think that you need to know. We'll talk about sell-almost-anything sites with site-specific information and all the details needed to decide how and where to list your stuff. I'll give you tips on selling through in-person avenues with advice on accepting digital payments.

As promised, the last part of the text will go into detail on all of the sites listed previously in the book.

First, we will cover the sell-almost-anything sites that literally sell almost anything.

Then, the category-specific sites will follow.

Sell-almost-anything Sites

These sites have the widest possible audience and, therefore, the best chances of you finding a buyer within your price range in an expeditious manner.

You will have to expect to get a little less than you would if you were able to utilize a site that is totally devoted to your item. But the slight monetary loss you might see is made up for in time.

I myself believe that pretty much anything can be replaced, except for time and life. So, for me, it's an easy decision – time over money. That's easy to say when I do not have and have not had too many things that could be considered valuable. It makes life a little easier that way.

Small wants and needs equate to simpler happiness, easy gratitude for non-material things.

I digress, but the point is, it will always come down to how much time and effort you are able and willing to put into your selling endeavor.

Everyone has their own way of doing things, and the same will apply to how you choose to go about letting go of all your stuff.

I personally prefer the platforms that allow me to find a buyer online and then meet them in person. The ones I have used the most are craigslist and Facebook. In the interest of being transparent, it has to be noted that there is a different element of danger when you have to meet with someone in person rather than completely online, but we will talk about that later in the safety section.

The list below is in alphabetical order so as to show no partiality and provide information so that you can make the best decision for yourself.

5miles – In short, you create an account, take a picture of your item, list the item according to its category, and 5miles will instantly match you with buyers in your area, according to your GPS location. You can join for free, but there is a 10% service fee whenever an item sells. You will need to meet with your buyer, but there is some security in the fact that 5miles implements a phone verification process that other sites like craigslist do not.

Bonanza – On this site, you can't sell almost anything, but the possibilities are still numerous. Their list of categories includes almost all of your stuff except tools and vehicles. This platform is more like eCommerce, where you will sign up for free and create your own online store with your products. Bonanza boasts of an involved, readily available support team, special links with the major online selling platforms, and savvy buyers who are drawn back in for repeat sales.

Craigslist – Oh my, I have some stories about craigslist, but I have no space here, and some of them are just way inappropriate. Anyhow, basically, it is one of the simplest sites to use. You click a link to create a posting, choose the category, upload your pictures, write your description, specify your location and other pertinent details, and then wait until you are contacted. You can choose to only communicate through a craigslist generic email, or you can include your name, email, and/or phone number. You make contact with the interested party, make arrangements and sell your stuff. While simple and free, you have to be cautious of scammers and the real danger that can and has happened.

eBay – An oldie but goodie – eBay. It connects you with buyers without having to actually meet them. It is free to get started, and eBay will let you list up to 50 items for free a month and then .30 per item after that. There are several selling options, including an auction and fixed price. There is a massive audience looking for a huge range of items on eBay. EBay will help you with postage and shipping from home, and they claim to help you get up to 25% off those costs. The bottom line is that there is a 10% final value fee on anything you sell, whether it is three dollars or three thousand dollars.

eBid – While eBid and eBay sound very similar, there are some structural differences. While eBid does not charge listing fees, they do charge a final value fee of 3 percent. The site totes the title of the 2019 best value online auction site award and literally sells pretty much anything. All selling options start off standard with no listing fees and a final value fee maximum of 5%. There are other optional upgrades that you may want to invest in that helps you and your buyer connect. Additionally, before you can begin to sell on eBid, you will need to have a form of payment on file and verified.

Etsy – It calls itself a creative marketplace and therefore caters to both buyers and sellers who are selling items that can be classified as creative in nature. You basically set up a store to list your items, so this option is great for those who have a huge collection of creative type items. Selling them here will get you a faster buyer for a better price. There is a .20 listing fee per item, a 5% transaction fee, and a 3% and .25 payment processing fee. So, along with fetching a more sophisticated buyer who will pay more for what you have, you will also have to commit to paying for that reputation and exposure.

Everything But the House – This interesting and unique concept works differently than your typical selling avenues. Rather than offering the sellers either a platform to list their items or the option of creating an online store, this site wants to do it for you. Whether you are literally selling everything in your house, a small collection of items, or just a few things, they want to take over for you and get your stuff sold.

Basically, you indicate the number of items you have and the frequency you want to sell, select the categories that your items belong to, specify whether you are selling your own items from home or you are a professional, such as a collector or dealer, send photos, provide an email and then a representative from the site contacts you to discuss your possibilities. Of course, this level of sophistication and service will come with a price tag, but it takes the burden off of you in every way and allows a team of pros to tackle the challenge for you.

Facebook marketplace and groups – There are two options when it comes to selling items through Facebook: using marketplace or as a member of a Facebook group. Both are completely free to use; you can list as many items as you want, you have a massive audience, and Facebook, like the other paid sites, also includes tips and advice for how to best use their site. Of course, you will have to have a Facebook profile in order to use either option, which is comforting to many people because a person's social media page can tell you a lot about them. To publish an item on the marketplace, in your news feed, you click marketplace, follow the simple instructions, and publish your post in the marketplace. To use the group option, you will need to join a group that is devoted to selling. There are some that are garage sale style and some that are very specific and focused. Once you are a member of that group, you post your item and go from there.

Letgo – Letgo is similar to other sites that ask you to create posts according to the items' category and then connects both parties together according to distance. You create an account using a social media handle or your email and then use that account to set up your selling posts. It is completely free to use, with no listing fees, membership, or payment fees. Being that this site is focused on secondhand selling with no specialty focus, you can expect to get a little less than you might elsewhere. On the upside, it is free and easy to use.

Mercari – I have seen a lot of advertisements for this site in the past several months. The site states that it has a very simple process – you list it, you ship it, and then you get paid. Now, of course, there is some fine print associated with each one of those steps, but the goal is to make it as easy as possible on the seller and the buyer. There is a flat 10% selling fee that will be accrued for every item that is sold. Mercari has some policies in place that help both parties to have a smooth, profitable experience. Once the item sells, the buyer packages it with a shipping label that is sent to them via email from mercari; the seller is responsible for getting the package shipped within 3 business days, and then the seller confirms that the purchase has been dropped off for shipment. These simple steps hold sellers accountable and help to uphold mercari's reputation.

Nextdoor – It is similar to craigslist in the sense that it is free and aims to connect people who are local to one another. The process is simple, and a step by step guide easily walks you through it. While not as well known or as widely used as craigslist, it is a great additional option to use when selling your stuff. The more platforms that you use, the greater your exposure, the faster your item will sell for the best possible price. A really nice option included on nextdoor is the ability to directly benefit local nonprofits and help the local community.

Offerup – While I myself have not used offerup extensively, my younger sister has and has had great success. You sign up for the app, create an account, create a listing, connect with a buyer, and then arrange to meet up. There may be some people who use offerup and then post the items without having to meet, but those are rare. Be ready to meet people when using this app because that is its sole focus – connecting interested parties who are in the same vicinity. It is free and easy to use, just please make sure to be very safe anytime you are meeting anyone in public.

Oodle – This site fancies itself as an online classified ads platform that uses social media to connect people who are looking to buy, sell, and trade. Not as well known or used as the other more popular sites, it can be a good additional place to post your listings for maximum exposure. All you need to do is create an account, and then you can get started immediately. Beware, the site has a rudimentary look. That, coupled with the fact that it is a free service not so widely used, means you may end up with garage sale minded buyers.

Varagesale – The biggest selling point for using this app is that everyone has to go through a manual review process before they are allowed to buy or sell. This alone makes it worth taking a look at. The chances of someone trying to harm you or take from you dwindle down to nil when they know that their real personal information is documented along with your transaction history. It is completely free to use and is linked with Facebook. Because it utilizes Facebook as its connecting point, it authenticates your buyers. Like its name, you have to remember that you will be looking to get garage sale dollar amounts.

Category-specific Sales Sites

Category-specific sites will make a big difference in finding the ideal buyer who is willing to pay the optimum price.

The whole purpose of a site that focuses on one category or a small collection of them is to cater to parties on both sides who have a common interest.

An individual who has a passion for collecting antiques is

much more likely to pay top dollar for certain items on a category-specific site than the opposite. The opposite is a person who has a general interest in a certain type of item but does not have the drive to spend more money on items that a collector or connoisseur would.

With the category-specific sites, there will be different fees that the sellers and buyers will have to invest in. Additionally, it can be a long process because while the site is dedicated to certain types of items and market to that demographic, you are still marketing to a narrower buying population.

Again, it always comes down to how much time, effort, and money you are able and willing to invest and the lowest dollar amount you will accept.

Chapter 10: Items to Let Go: What Should I Sell?

There is a market out there to sell almost anything, and I do mean almost anything. At some point, you either bought an item or thought enough of it to hold onto it. Now is the time to pass it on to its next loving owner.

The A to Z list below offers some suggestions for things to sell, followed by detailed definitions of the category and tips on how to sell the item. Each category will have a list of options to sell both on and offline. The next section of the text will have detailed information about the selling avenues. There will be information about the websites where you can sell almost anything, such as eBay, Amazon, Facebook, and craigslist. In addition, each category will have item specific sites.

Some things are automatic, easy sellers, and some things take a little more effort and time to find a purchaser, but there is also another you that is on the lookout and will take it off your hands. Will you always get the amount of money in the timeframe you were looking for? Of course not. If that were the case, we would be living in a more perfect world, and that is not what is going on. However, there are more options than you might think. Over the years, I have sold all kinds of things, from the most 'necessary' items such as vehicles, lawnmowers, kitchen utensils, and appliances, to the not so necessary such as American eagle figurines, fur coats, and doilies for craft projects. Like everything, it is just a matter of having the right information and then the right plan.

The next section of the book has detailed information on all of the websites listed for each category. For the offline options, there is a section for tips on how to organize those sales, tips for safe selling, and other useful details.

Look around you and then take a look at the list below to see what it is that you have to sell:

Antiques	Appliances	Art	Baby gear
Books	CDs and DVDs	Clothing	Collectibles
Craft Supplies	Décor	Electronics	Furniture
Gift Cards	Housewares	Jewelry	Kids' Stuff
Musical Instruments	Office	Outdoor and gardening	Pet
School Supplies	Sports gear and memorabilia	Tools	Vehicles
Video Games	Vintage	Yard and lawn equipment	

Antiques

To be considered an antique, an item should be at least 100 years old, though this is not a hard and fast rule, and the item can be considered valuable because of its considerable age.

When you have decided to let an antique item go, there are some things to keep in mind.

First and foremost, do your research thoroughly. When you know what you have, what it is potentially worth, the potential purchase price, the options for selling it, and then the turnaround time for the sale, you are better equipped to get started.

Additionally, make sure that you research how and where you are going to sell your item. That is the next most important aspect after knowing exactly what you have.

To get started, really get to know your item. It may be that painting that you got from dear Aunt Stella twenty years ago that has been stored in the attic since 2002, or the set of books you yourself bought at an estate sale and have had on your dresser, unread, since then. No matter what it is, being that it is an antique, you want to take some extra time to investigate and arm yourself with information.

There are five key things to consider: age, condition, current demand, provenance, and rarity.

Age - You will need to determine the age of the item first because, well, that is what determines whether or not it is truly an antique. An entire book could be written on how to determine if the item you have is truly an antique.

There are a couple of general points to keep in mind: 1) Classify the object so that you can narrow down your search. Once you do your search, that alone may be able to give you your answer. 2) Look for signs that it is handmade. Hand stitching marks created by hand tools and a subtle lack of symmetry are all signs that something was handmade and therefore more likely to be an antique. 3) If possible, look for a patent number and then use this link to verify:
http://patft.uspto.gov/netahtml/PTO/srchnum.htm

Condition – Is the item in good condition and well preserved? Of course, the better shape it is in and in its original state, the more it will be worth. Whatever the condition is, be sure to clearly communicate that with your buyer(s) beforehand.

Current demand – Anyone who has watched their share of Antiques Roadshow knows that the demand and value of antiques fluctuate as needs and situations change. Right now, the United States is battling the coronavirus and dealing with social issues. Those conditions alone will change the demand.

Provenance – What a pretty word; it looks and feels like an old Puritan girls' name. What it means is the chronology of ownership of an item. If you already have or can obtain the recording of the history of your item, it will automatically have more value and authenticity.

Rarity – Supply and demand. If you have something that there is not a lot of and there is at least a small market for it, you have the upper hand. Therefore, it is crucial to know exactly what it is that you have.

If you find it difficult to identify and find the valuation of your item, there are some websites that can help give you more detailed information and walk you through the process.

https://www.worthpoint.com/

https://antiques.lovetoknow.com/Main_Page

https://www.justanswer.com/sip/antiques

https://www.whatsellsbest.com/research/prices/antiques.php

If you have antique books that you want to sell, check out the Antiquarian Booksellers' Association of America (ABAA) https://www.abaa.org/about-abaa/how-to-join. Being a very studious and reputable entity, their membership requirements are selective, specific, and only proven, professional applicants who meet the criteria are allowed. While you may not qualify to sell on this site, there is a plethora of information on how to determine the value of a book, authenticating autographs, valuating old Bibles, and other valuable insight.

Where to sell your antiques online:

Amazon - https://www.amazon.com/

Bonanza - https://www.bonanza.com/sell_products_online

eBay - https://www.ebay.com/b/Antiques

Craigslist - https://houston.craigslist.org/search/ata

Etsy - https://www.etsy.com/market/antique

Everything but the house - https://sell.ebth.com/

Facebook auction and marketplace - https://www.facebook.com/marketplace/

https://www.facebook.com/liveauctionsandsales/

Go Antiques - https://www.goantiques.com/sign-up-for-goantiques

Mercari - https://www.mercari.com/

Morphy's Auctions - https://www.morphyauctions.com/consigning/

Replacements - https://www.replacements.com/sell-to-us/

Ruby Lane - https://www.rubylane.com/

Shopify - https://www.shopify.com/

Sotheby's - https://www.sothebys.com/en/sell?locale=en

Specialty sites – Identify your item and then search for a site that specializes in that category. They will have up to date, specific information, and hopefully, get you a price close to what you are looking for.

TIAS - https://www.tias.com/

Go Antiques – This is a good option to utilize if you have a house full of antiques or just a serious interest in them and want to continue to buy and sell antiques. There are three basic packages you can choose from – basic, professional, and power. The basic membership is $24.99 per month and allows a seller to post up to 100 items. The professional package is $49.99 per month, allows up to 1,000 items along with 10 free item features per month. Lastly, the power package is $74.99 and allows up to 1,000,000 item listings and 10 free item features a month. If you have enough inventory or valuable enough stuff, this may be a good option for your antiques.

Morphy's Auctions – This community utilizes auctions where the highest bidder will take the prized item up for sale. With this platform, you will need to place your item(s) in consignment. That basically means that they will sell your item and take an agreed-upon amount of the sale price when it is sold at auction. This is a process for the savvy antique buying and selling population who have valuable stock. To get started, you will need to make contact with a representative to have your items valued. You can meet them at their gallery, email the information, use the website, mail in your photos and information, or visit them at one of their shows to begin the process.

Replacements – Any and all high-end antique dinnerware, glassware, flatware, and collectibles can be bought and sold here. It specializes in replacing missing items in a collector's set and uses sellers to find these replacements. Using their website, you will need to positively identify exactly what pattern and kind of wares you have. Once it is identified, you send in a form with pictures of your items, and the site will contact you with a quote.

Ruby Lane – Ruby Lane lists its top five selling categories of items as jewelry, dolls, porcelain and pottery, silver, and art. This site is listed under antiques because most of the items listed in the above categories are high-end antiques. Being that they are working with items in a higher price range to a more exclusive clientele, you should expect higher fees, more listing rules, and a more detailed process to sign up.

All Ruby Lane 'shops' must have at least 10 items available for purchase at all times, offer at least one online payment method, and there is a maintenance fee of

$54 per month, allowing up to 50 items to be listed per month. This is a great option for those who have a large inventory of valuable items to get to the buyer who has the desire and the funds to invest.

Sotheby's – This antique auction house has over 275 years of experience in selling only the most high-quality, rarest antiques in the industry. Sotheby's claims to make the process very easy for the seller in 4 easy steps: 1) Submit photographs of the item(s), 2) Provide as much information as possible, including dimensions, history, and documentation, 3) Review the pictures and details, then submit, and 4) Let Sotheby's handle the rest in an auction. Since they are an antique authority and are taking on all of the work, it to be reasonably expected that you will pay for that convenience and expertise.

Where to sell your antiques offline/in person:

Antique Mall

Antique show

Auctions

Consignment shop

Estate Sale

Flea Market

Garage Sale

Antique dealer

Appliances

There is an appliance for almost every function of life at this point. While the biggest, most essential appliances are the most sought after and the big-ticket items, there is plenty of boutique and single-use appliances that can be rehomed. If you can't get rid of the fridge, how about that personal pie maker you got two Christmases ago or the donut maker your aunt gave you for your wedding?

Realistically, your options on whether or not to sell your item online or in-person will be limited by how large the item is and if it makes sense to ship it. Large appliances like stoves and refrigerators cost too much to ship, so you would have to sell these in person.

Everything in the home that plugs into an outlet and serves a purpose can be called an appliance. Personally, I would only make these sales online just because shipping becomes such an issue. Smaller items that are not high-end will not fetch a price worth the hassle and cost of shipping. With the larger items, the cost and hassle to ship them negate the possibility of a profit from the sale.

In my experience, the best way to sell a used appliance, especially during this whole pandemic situation, is to utilize an online platform, find your buyer, follow safety guidelines, meet your buyer in a public place, and make the sale.

There are some tips to keep in mind when you get ready to sell your appliance(s) using an online platform:

Take plenty of high-quality photos showing the item from all angles and if there are any flaws, make sure to capture those close. This will save a lot of time answering questions, or even worse, meeting a buyer, and then the sale being canceled.

The dimensions of the appliance are crucial. Even if it is just a microwave, a toaster oven, blender, etc., you need to know its exact size. Measure the height, width, length, and have the information on how much it holds and stores. Everyone has different living situations and needs and may have specific requirements they are looking for. Arming yourself and supplying your potential buyers with as much information as possible will help you get the most out of your sale and find the right buyer faster.

When creating your ad, post, or sale notification – use an attention-grabbing headline. For example – "Refrigerator for sale $200" leaves a lot of room for questions, does not draw attention, and is easy to scroll right past. In contrast – "Side-by-side Frigidaire, 1-year old refrigerator, a steal at only $200" gives your audience some much-needed details, showcases its qualities, and invites more attention. If you are questioning what you should say, scroll through other similar ads, compare the condition, pricing, and wording to help guide you.

Specify your location. For example, I live near Houston,

Texas. For those of you who don't know, Houston is the largest city in Texas, the third-largest in the United States, and home to almost two and a half million people. The reason I mention this is because I live in the country, 45 miles northeast of Houston. While this is considered close to us Houstonians, it is really far from most other non-Texans and non-Houstonians. Be clear with your selling audience about where you are located and exactly where you are willing to meet.

Where to sell your appliances online:

5miles - https://www.5miles.com/a/home-appliances

Craigslist - https://houston.craigslist.org/search/ppa

eBay - https://www.ebay.com/b/Major-Appliances-Parts-Accessories

Facebook marketplace - https://www.facebook.com/marketplace/

Letgo - https://www.letgo.com/en-us/i/appliances-galore-and-so-much-more

Mercari - https://www.mercari.com/us/category/668/

OfferUp - https://offerup.com/explore/k/appliances/

While this list is for the online option to make sales, the reality is that you will still need to meet with people to do the actual transaction.

See the section about safe selling online and in person.

Where to sell your appliances offline:

Appliance resellers

Classified ads

Garage/Yard sales

Local appliance sales

Pawnshops

Scrap metal recyclers

Art

Most people have some form of art in their homes. Whether it's a painting, a drawing, sculpture, enamelwork, furniture design, a mosaic, or some other form of art, most of us have some sort of art in our homes.

Just like anything else, whether you are going to sell your art is dependent upon your need and your attachment to the item.

I am not a connoisseur of art, nor anything close to a collector. The "art" I have in my house would not be hard for me to part with, with the exception of the pieces my daughter has created. Those are from the heart and a piece of my amazing grown baby, so there is no way that I would get rid of them.

The art I would be able to get rid of would probably be considered décor rather than art.

So, the question becomes, what is the difference between art and décor? Art is meant to have a deeper purpose or meaning that is related to the receiver of the message through its arrangement of color, texture, shape, and other elements. On the other hand, décor is less meaningful. Décor's purpose is to fill a space, embellish an area, or help to enhance other objects around it.

When thinking about selling your art, the most important thing to remember is that it is dependent on what other people are willing to pay for it and what the buying climate is at the time you try to sell it.

Where to sell your art online:

Artfire - https://www.artfire.com/

Artplode - https://www.artplode.com/

eBay - https://www.ebay.com/b/Art

Etsy - https://www.etsy.com/market/art

Facebook marketplace:
https://www.facebook.com/marketplace/

Artfire – Specializing in custom/hand made items, this site requires the seller to set up a 'shop' and offers three shop options: Standard Shop - $4.95 per month, .23 per listing item fee, 12.75% final valuation fee, and allows up to 250 active items to be listed. The Popular Shop is $20.00 per month, 4.5% final valuation fee, and allows up to 1,000 active listings. The Featured Shop is $40.00 per month, 4.5% final valuation fee, with up to 2500 active listings. For any of the shop options, Artfire states that they offer promotional tools, low cost, and community and education to make the most of your shop. I would recommend browsing the other items they have to sell to see if you would have a place there and then decide which shop option works for you.

Artplode – Art is sold here from artists selling their own original work, dealers/galleries selling works for different artists, and private sellers selling works that they own. The FAQ states that they charge a "low flat one-off fee," and that information becomes available after you register with Artplode. They claim that this one-off fee saves both the buyer and the seller money because they do not charge a commission percentage to the buyer and seller the way an auction does. It leaves the decision of how to assign the shipping costs up to the seller. Some sellers decide to absorb packaging and shipping costs; others require the buyer to take care of these costs. I would say, get a quote from an entity that offers them for free and then compare it to the efforts and cost you would see here.

I find all expressions of art to be valuable, but we live in a world where works have assigned values depending on many variables. That being said, if your items are not considered rare or high end, try using one of the sell-almost-anything sites.

Where to sell your art offline:

Art auction

Art gallery

Festival

Flea market

Garage/yard sale

Baby Gear

They grow up so fast. Before you know it, they're walking. It seems like just yesterday, mine were that small.

All new parents hear some version of these statements. It is true that the littles go through rapid transformations in a very short amount of time, from birth to three years old. What is also true is that they need a lot of stuff to make it through that time.

What your small person needed when they were two weeks old is much different than what they needed when they get to be two years old.

Rather than hold onto these outgrown items, if they are in good condition, they can help fetch you a pretty penny.

The usual items are always going to be in demand. Bassinets, cribs, any type of baby carrier, strollers, bedding, car seats, playpens, baby monitors, toys, and of course, clothes, blankets, and bibs. Not to mention the plethora of new items that come out on a regular basis.

Selling baby items is the same as selling any other type of item in the sense that you have to know what you are selling, you have to know your market, and go with the best platform or avenue for you.

Where it differs is that most parents of the small people are going to be a little more critical and questioning because the item is contributing to the care of the most vulnerable of us, the babies.

When it comes to anything fabric, it needs to be as clean as possible. No one wants to put anything stained or funny, smelling next to their child's skin. Be sure to disinfect and clean everything you have for the best possible pictures and sales.

The other important thing to consider is that some items such as car seats, strollers, playpens, bouncers, etc., that babies and toddlers play with and move in can sometimes be recalled.

No one wants to buy or sell something that has had a product recall issued. If an item was recalled, it is for a good reason. It means that at some time, there was enough evidence of a child being harmed because of the object that it had to be removed from the market.

Use these sites to check and see if the item you are thinking of selling has had a safety recall issued for it:

United States Consumer Product Safety Commission: https://www.cpsc.gov/Recalls

USA Government Recalls: https://www.usa.gov/recalls

Parents' magazine: https://www.parents.com/product-recalls/

Where to sell your baby items online:

Facebook marketplace and Facebook groups:

https://www.facebook.com/marketplace/

https://www.facebook.com/groups/feed/

ThredUP: https://www.thredup.com/

Craigslist: https://houston.craigslist.org/search/baa

Kid to Kid: https://kidtokid.com/

eBay: https://www.ebay.com/b/Baby-Gear

Josies Friends: https://josiesfriends.com/

OfferUp: https://offerup.com/explore/k/baby-kids/

Kidizen: https://kidizen.com/

Swoondle Society: https://www.swoondlesociety.com/

ThredUP: The items sold here are clothing and accessory oriented, with sections for maternity and kids. The initial process is simple enough:

1) order a clean out kit and fill it with high-quality brands

2) send it to Thredup

3) get paid when your items sell.

This site essentially just asks you to send in your items, and they handle the rest.

Their listing process for your items:

a) 12-point quality inspection

b) Professional photographs

c) Write detailed descriptions

d) They ship your items to buyers once they sell

The important things to remember:

1) They are very selective and only accept 40% of items received. If your item is accepted but not sold within 7 days, you must reclaim the item, or it becomes property of Thredup

2) Any items that are accepted are classified as either value and mall brands and have a 60-day listing window, or they are classed as premium and designer brands and

have a 90-day listing

3) (and possibly the most important thing to know) – "Your payout is a percentage of thredUP's selling price." The higher the price of the item, the higher your payout percentage. The lowest, $5.00-$19.99, receives a 5-15% payout, and the higher range, $200.00+, sees a payout of 80% with varying payout percentages in between.

Josie's Friends: This is a consignment site where you will earn 50% of the sale price, payable via PayPal 15-30 days from the transaction date. They like to keep the process simple and take the work off your hands. You request a consigner bag, send your best items in, and then Josie's Friends will prep, photograph, and market your items for you. In the interest of keeping it simple, their site states that they are looking for quality rather than brand names. The quality items are baby, children, juniors, women's, maternity, footwear, and handbags. Their acceptance policy is that the items be of high quality, freshly laundered, no stains or smells, all fastening elements must be in working order, have a brand and size tag, and all seasons and brands are accepted year-round as long as they are not off-price or outdated. To get started or for more information, use the form provided on the site to make an inquiry.

Kidizen: Kidizen has the right idea for all the busy mamas of the world – make it clear and easy. Their listed categories they specialize in are baby, girl, boy, and mama. There are two options to sell with Kidizen, you can create a listing by creating an account, or you can let one of their style scouts do it for you. There is a 12% fee deducted and a .50 marketplace fee deduction from every item sold. All sellers are responsible for the shipping costs and are paid for the item once it ships. To help you achieve selling success, Kidizen has tips and guidance for setting up shop, order management, listing tips, photography advice, inside information on seasonality and when best to sell your items, shipping hints, a seller corner community to interact with other sellers, an extensive FAQ section, and an app for selling ease for buyer and seller.

Swoondle Society: You cannot sell your items here. Instead, you trade your items in and use the 'trade balances' to purchase other items for sale. While you won't get cash with this site, you will be able to send in the baby and kid's clothing that they have outgrown and pick something out that works for them now. Even though there is no monetary return, the value is in using the outgrown items to bring in new ones. You request a kit, which is $5, that comes with a prepaid shipping bag, and $5 swoondle credit – so you immediately break even. Send your items in, swoondle places a value on your items assigns a trade balance to your account, and then you trade out within your level. Lastly, you will need to become a member and pick a trading plan.

Where to sell your baby items offline:

Consignment stores

Garage/yard sales

Once Upon a Child

Children's Orchard

Books

If you are a reader, chances are that you either have way too many books now, or you have had too many at some point.

I am now and always have been an avid reader. I believe that the written and spoken word is the most powerful tool we have at our ready disposal.

It is how we communicate, learn, share, grow, practice our chosen religions, and basically grow as humans on an individual and collective level.

The books that have the most value are limited edition, first edition, and collectible; old and rare books; textbooks; autographed books; encyclopedias; niche hardcover books; cookbooks; graphic novels; and sheet music.

Paperback fiction, or mind candy, as I like to call them, can be sold piece by piece or in bulk. Selling them piece by piece can be very time consuming and eat up your profit. Try to sell them as a bulk lot. You may get a little less than you would have if you had sold them piece by piece, but it typically will take a lot less time.

When trying to determine the possible listing price of your book, try these two sites.

You will need to locate the ISBN number of the book, enter it into the fields on the sites, and you will get a general idea of what you can expect for your book.

Direct Textbook: https://www.directtextbook.com/

Flipsy: https://flipsy.com/sell-textbooks

Where to sell your books online –

Barnes and Nobles: https://www.barnesandnoble.com/textbook/textbook-buyback.jsp

Book Scouter: https://bookscouter.com/

Book Monster: https://www.chegg.com/sell-textbooks

Amazon (as a third party seller): https://www.amazon.com/sell-products-online

Chegg: https://www.chegg.com/sell-textbooks

Sell back your book: http://www.sellbackyourbook.com/

Bookstores.com: https://www.bookstores.com/

Cash 4 Books: https://www.cash4books.net/

Textbook Rush: https://www.textbookrush.com/

Barnes and Nobles: Short and sweet – they only want your textbooks. Enter the ISBN to get a quote, they ship you a prepaid label, you send the book(s) in, and then you are sent a check if the book is in acceptable condition and is valued at $10.00 or more.

Book Scouter: Textbooks and used books are both accepted. Enter the ISBN to search through over 30+ buyback vendors, compare the pricing and seller feedback on the possible vendors, and then ship your book in and wait to get paid. The vendor that you choose will determine when you get paid. Typically, payment is issued 1-3 days after receiving and checking your shipment. The fastest payment is through PayPal, but if you prefer to get a check in the mail, it will take an additional 3-7 days to reach you.

Book Monster: You can sell your used books, textbooks, CD's and DVD's here. Another fairly simple process here: 1) look up your item with an ISBN, barcode, title, author, etc. though ISBN works best, 2) Go to the 'buyback cart' to add titles to your cart, 3) Assess the condition of the item(s) using their condition guidelines, update the condition, click 'buyback checkout.' You will need either 10 items or $10 value before going to shipping and checkout, 4) Finally, enter your shipping and payment information and 'submit buyback.' Of note – if your item is received and is not found as acceptable and you choose to have the item returned to you, you will be responsible for the cost of shipping.

GoTextbooks: Use the ISBN to get a quote on your textbook, ship to gotextbooks, get paid. Once the books are received, they are processed within 5 business days. Once the book is accepted, there are two payment options. If you request a check to be mailed, delivery takes about 7-14 days. Using PayPal means that payments are posted within 2-14 days of acceptance. Take a look at grading guidelines specifications and what qualifies as an unacceptable or auto-reject book to ensure that it meets standards.

Bookstores.com: With this site, you are able to sell textbooks, movies, TV shows, and video games. For the textbooks, the seller creates an account in the marketplace, set up payment details, and then upload your inventory. The site states that they are not accepting new sellers in the marketplace right now, but that is always subject to change. There is a 15% commission that comes out of the sale price of the book, and the shipping credits are issued to the seller. For the movies, TV, and video games selling, you search for your item to get a quote, print the prepaid shipping label to send it in for free, and then get paid in-store credit, by check, or with PayPal.

Cash 4 Books: In addition to buying textbooks, this site also uses the Example 500 list to show what other kinds of books they buy. A quick perusal of these lists shows that these texts may not be classified as textbooks but are still educational in nature, must be 2017 or newer, and is subject to demand and inventory. I reread this next part at least 4 times to verify I was seeing it correctly. There are NO fees to use this site – at all. The service is free, free price quotes, and free shipping. Search for the ISBN, use the free shipping label to send the books in, and receive payment with a check or through PayPal. It typically takes 13 days from the time you hit 'sell my books' to when payment is issued. After the payment is processed, it is sent within one business day. If you submit an item that is not accepted, it can be sent back to the seller for the shipping expense; if it is not claimed within 14 days, the item is then used at the site's discretion.

For antique books – see the antique section of this text, or visit ABAA (Antiquarian Booksellers' Association of America) https://www.abaa.org/about-antiquarian-books/faq for information, direction, and insight.

Where to sell your books offline

Garage/Yard sales

Half Priced books

Local bookstore

CDs and DVDs

Now that Netflix, Hulu, Prime, AppleTV, IMDB, YouTube, Pandora, Spotify, iCloud, and others are available to provide everyone with their music and movie needs, most of us don't have the need or desire to hold onto that CD or DVD collection.

At this point, I have a small collection of DVDs that I use when my internet goes out and a handful of kid classics that you can never go wrong with when you have a visitor who is under the age of ten.

Because these items are lightweight and easy to ship, you may want to take advantage of that and sell them online.

The biggest thing to keep in mind when selling CDs and

DVDs is to make sure you are only selling items in top condition. You know, no scratches, plays through without skipping or stopping, and optimally, in its original case with the original artwork cover.

Where to sell your CDs and DVDs online:

Decluttr: https://www.decluttr.com/

FYE: https://www.decluttr.com/

Eagle Saver: https://www.eaglesaver.com/

Bonavendi: https://www.bonavendi.com/

Sell DVDs Online: http://www.selldvdsonline.com/

eBay: https://www.ebay.com/b/Music-CDs

Craigslist: https://houston.craigslist.org/search/emd

Facebook Marketplace: https://www.facebook.com/marketplace/

Decluttr: With this site, you can sell CDs, DVDs, games, textbooks, cell phones, and some tech products like kindles and wearables. First, you get an instant valuation by searching for your item using barcodes or details on your tech item. You will have 10 days to confirm the details of your order, and the valuation offered is good for 28 days. Then, you will carefully pack your items, print out a free shipping label, and then send it out. Once the items are received at the warehouse, the items will be examined, any personal electronic information scrubbed and set up for payment. If your item is deemed unacceptable, it will be recycled by the site at no cost to you. You get paid the next day via direct deposit or PayPal. You also have the option of donating your proceeds to charity. For an order to be complete and payment issued, it must either have 10 media items or be worth over $5.

Eagle Saver: The types of items that this site buys are books, CDs, DVDs, and video games. This free site and aims to make the process simple and profitable. You get a quote using the ISBN or UPC code on the item. Once your quote is created and the order completed, you have 5 business days to postmark the package using the free shipping label. After the package arrives, usually about 1-6 business days, payment is sent through a check or PayPal within 1 business day. If Eagle Saver is unable to accept an item, you will receive an email with an explanation, and the item will be shipped back to you for free.

Bonavendi: Acting as a third party, this site takes the information you supply about your item, CDs, DVDs, books, or video games, to match you with over 30+ vendors who buy the type of item you are trying to sell. A number of factors determine each vendor's buyback pricing, including inventory, condition guidelines, and demand. Once you have selected the vendor, bonavendi says they will guide you through the selling process, and you get paid a few days after the item has shipped. There is some crucial information not readily available, probably because it is vendor-specific – like fees, policies, and exact details—just a heads up.

Sell DVDs Online: There is a seemingly easy three-step process:

1) Get a quote for your DVD, CD, or games using the UPC

2) Print out the free shipping label and send it in

3) Get paid check or PayPal

The site says that you get paid within 3 days of receipt of the item. While they do strive to issue payment quickly, they acknowledge that by using USPS media mail, it can take up to 21 days to reach the warehouse, and once received, the goal is to get it checked within one business day.

Where to sell your CDs and DVDs offline:

Garage/Yard Sales

Local Bookstore

Reseller

Pawn Shop

Clothing

Big and small. Short and tall. There is someone out there who can use it all. Rhyme done.

Clothing is not always the easiest way to make cash, but the potential is there, depending on what you have.

Before the pandemic came at the beginning of 2020, one of my favorite things to do was to visit thrift stores and garage sales to find a new-to-me outfit.

Having been on the poorer side of things for as long as I can remember, I found joy in hand-me-downs and secondhand clothes. They were pieces that had been loved before and were more likely to be unique and eclectic, something I value.

There is another way to look at this too. Without realizing it, when we continuously buy more and more clothes, we are contributing to the world's level of waste and therefore helping to raise the levels of toxicity and pollution.

So, what kind of clothing items do you have that you can let go of?

Are you like me with a wardrobe largely made up of gently worn, previously loved, second life clothing?

Or do you have a closet full of brand-new clothes and shoes – some still with tags on them?

And, of course, the majority probably fall somewhere in between.

Whoever you are, there is a shopping population just like you out there somewhere looking for something they like and ideally looks as good on them as they imagined.

When selling your clothes, here are some pointers to help you along the way:

People want two things in clothing, for it to fit properly and look good. You can help them by taking multiple, detailed pictures and having accurate measurements. If it is a name brand, go to their website to pull up a copy of their sizing guide and include it with the picture so that your buyer has an accurate idea of what size they will be with that particular brand. Also, I include a picture of myself in it (if it still fits) and then include my size compared to the item that I am listing.

For unique, handmade, and specialty items, it is very important to take all of the measurements, not just list the size. The sizing can vary, especially if it were ever altered, as would be the case for formal and bridal wear.

If you bought the item recently, you could find an image online and include it with your pictures to show how much it currently goes for new.

No one wants a new-to-them piece of clothing that is missing a button or has a stain that can be removed. Bring your item to its prime condition by mending, cleaning, ironing, and displaying properly before taking pictures or selling in person.

Be realistic and fair when deciding on pricing. Don't go too low and undervalue your item, but at the same time, you cannot expect to get back what you paid for it, even if it is a high-end brand name – it is still preowned.

If someone asks a question about a piece that you have in a private conversation, make sure to update your listing to include his information. If one person asks you something, chances are that someone else is wondering the same thing.

When shipping your items, something as simple as wrapping the clothing in tissue paper and including a small thank you note will entice the buyer to buy again.

Where to sell your clothes online –

thredUP - https://www.thredup.com/

Etsy - https://www.etsy.com/c/clothing

eBay - https://www.ebay.com/b/Womens-Clothing

The Real Real - https://www.therealreal.com/

Poshmark - https://poshmark.com/

Tradesy - https://www.tradesy.com/

ASOS Marketplace - https://marketplace.asos.com/my/boutiqueapplication/information

Crossroads - https://crossroadstrading.com/

Facebook marketplace and groups - https://www.facebook.com/marketplace/

https://www.facebook.com/groups/feed/

Mercari - https://www.mercari.com/

Buffalo Exchange - https://sellbymail.buffaloexchange.com/

Rebag - https://www.rebag.com/

ThredUP: The items sold here are clothing and accessory oriented. The initial process is simple enough:

1) Order a cleanout kit and fill it with high-quality brands

2) Send it to Thredup

3) Get paid when your items sell

This site essentially just asks you to send in your items, and they handle the rest. Their listing process for your items:

a) 12-point quality inspection, b) professional photographs, c) write detailed descriptions, d) they ship your items to buyers once they sell.

The important things to remember:

1) They are very selective and only accept 40% of items received. If your item is accepted but not sold within 7 days, you must reclaim the item, or it becomes property of Thredup

2) Any items that are accepted are classified as either value and mall brands and have a 60-day listing window, or they are classed as premium and designer brands and have a 90-day listing

3) (and possibly the most important thing to know) – "Your payout is a percentage of thredUP's selling price." The higher the price of the item, the higher your payout percentage. The lowest, $5.00-$19.99, receives a 5-15% payout, and the higher range, $200.00+ sees a payout of 80% with varying payout percentages in between

The Real Real – For the bourgeoisie. I jest. This is an online consignment shop specializing in designer and high-end brand name "women's and men's fashion, watches, fine jewelry, home décor, art, and kids' fashion." The top three fashion brands they consign are Chanel, Hermes, and Louis Vuitton. Any items must be in good condition (moderate wear) up to pristine condition (new with tags), and the site offers a Designer Directory to verify if your item is on the list.

For individual items listed and sold, their commission structure basically offers higher consignment percentages for higher sales. On the low end, anything that has a resale list price of $145 or less pays out 40% commission. The scale goes all the way up to watches with a resale list price of $2,495 or more with an 85% commission.

There is also a RealReal Rewards tier program where the commission amount and benefits increase as level and annual net sales increase. The insider level, $0 - $1,500 in sales, earns 55% of the selling price. Next, the icon level, $1,501 - $9,999 will net 60%. The top tier is the VIP level with $10,000 in sales, with 70% earned on the selling price and other benefits.

Overall, the consigning process is meant to be a basic 4 step process: 1) Verify that your item is on the designer list and decide what to consign, 2) Choose which consignment method you prefer: a) video chat consignment appointment with a luxury manager, b) video chat expert consultation about pricing watches, jewelry, and more, or c) ship your items direct for free with UPS. 3) Every item listed with TheRealReal is authenticated by a team of experts. 4) Get paid by direct deposit, site credit, which will net you an extra 5% each month, or have a check mailed to you. The commission structure is described above. There is also an option for an upfront sale rather than waiting for your item to sell before receiving any funds. The details for that process are available when you reach out to the site.

TheRealReal really does try to keep the process simple, but the fact is that there is a more rigorous structure and set of policies in place because they are dealing with a higher standard of items and, therefore, a higher monetary bracket.

Poshmark – Poshmark is a high-end resale site that wants to connect buyers and sellers in a more meaningful way than just the usual transactional relationship. While the option to search for a specific item or browse a category is there, there is an alternative focus on connecting buyers and sellers who have a common interest. Users are encouraged to "shop closets and boutiques ... [of] people whose style you adore". There are shopping parties 4 times a day hosted by various sellers with focused themes, such as 'best in maternity wear posh party' or 'everyday picks posh party.'

There is a lot going on with Poshmark, so take your time when assessing this site. Outside of the social interaction aspect, this site has some of the same basics as other resale sites. In theory, you should be able to list your items, ship them, and then get paid. The specifics on how this actually happens is scattered through various sections of the website and can be confusing. There is a 'sell on poshmark' field to click on where one would expect to get all the nitty-gritty on the process. Instead, you are just instructed to download the app.

After a little digging, I found out that the fees for Poshmark are: $2.95 for all sales under $15.00. Anything over $15.00, Poshmark takes a commission of 20%. These earnings become available after the buyer has received their item.

There is expedited shipping for all orders not weighing more than 5 pounds for $7.11 that is paid by the buyer.

I would say definitely take your time here when you are getting started. This site has a lot of positive feedback, but I can see where there may be some confusion for rookies.

Tradesy - What's notable with Tradesy is that they boast a claim of being a fashion marketplace, built by women, for women. This focus on women and fashion narrows their scope and, ideally, facilitates the buying and selling of bags, shoes, clothing, and other fashion items from top designers. The top-selling items are bags, accessories, shoes, and clothing.

Basically, you list your item(s) with pictures and details, set your price, confirm the order, and then ship it out.

There are three shipping options – shipping kit, prepaid label, or self-ship. Whichever option you choose, the cost of the shipping is added to the cost of the item, and the buyer pays both the listing price and the shipping. Once the item is shipped, your earnings will be in a pending status and may stay that way for up to 21 days after the item has been delivered to the buyer for security purposes.

Once you have made the sale, you now need to calculate the fees that will go to Tradesy.

For items less than $50.00, there is a flat rate of $7.50. Over $50.00, there is a 19.8% commission to Tradesy.

If you choose to spend your earnings on the Tradesy site, there are no additional fees.

In order to see that sale as cash, you will need to 'withdraw cash' to transfer your earnings from the tradesy account to your PayPal, debit card, or checking account, and there is a 2.9% safe transfer fee for this transaction. Transfers from the Tradesy account to the account of your choosing can take 7 or more business days to process.

The big picture here is that the process is pretty standard, and the fees /commissions are somewhere in the middle of the industry standard. The payment process is drawn out and longer than some would want to deal with, but its positive point is that it has a targeted audience for the higher-end women's' accessories, ensuring you will get top dollar for your items.

ASOS Marketplace - * vintage
https://marketplace.asos.com/my/boutiqueapplication/information

Crossroads - https://crossroadstrading.com/   * in person only

Buffalo Exchange -

https://sellbymail.buffaloexchange.com/ * in person only

Rebag – Designer handbags and accessories are the focus here. The Rebag process for selling luxury bags and accessories is fairly simple once you piece it together from various parts of the website.

Rebag only accepts certain designers, so you want to check their list, https://support.rebag.com/hc/en-us/articles/360039209512-What-designers-does-Rebag-accept- as your first step. Then the item will need to be submitted for authentication and approval. There are three ways to do this. 1) Submit through Clair. Rebag uses Clair, a luxury appraisal index, to determine an item's current resale value. It uses a formula to narrow down the specifics of your item. The critical information that Clair uses to begin the valuation process is identifying the bag to 'find your Clair code.' This formula looks at item type, designer, model, style, and size.

After this is determined, we move on to the grading process. This is used to determine the condition of the bag – grade A, excellent, grade B, great, grade C, very good, and grade D, good. The Clair grading system efficiently classifies exactly what item you have, what condition it is in, and then creates a value.

2) The second way to submit an item with Rebag is to visit a store in person. No appointment is necessary, and the quote should take about one hour to process.

3) As a final option, you are able to simply upload the photos of your item on the website or on the Rebag app. This is the longest of submission options and typically takes 1-2 business days to complete.

If you send in your items for submission with a shipping label and the item is not accepted, there is a $10 flat fee to ship the bag back.

After the item is submitted and the offer is given and accepted, it is now time to get the item to Rebag. That can be done in one of four ways, all free: a) courier pick up in Manhattan, b) prepaid shipping label, c) prepaid shipping box and label, d) drop off in person at a Rebag store.

Once the item is received, there is a vetting process that

takes 2-3 business days. After the item has been approved, the payment process will begin.

There are three options for getting paid – ACH electronic transfers, which you will see in your account in 1 full business day, a check that is issued within 2-7 business days to be delivered by mail, or Rebag credit is available at the completion of the order.

The pro of this site is that there are no fees or commissions taken out of your earnings. At least not as far as I could tell, and I combed through it extensively.

The con of this site is that there is no electronic payment option such as PayPal like there is for most other resale sites.

Where to sell your clothes offline –

Thrift store

Consignment shop

Garage/yard sale

Plato's Closet

Clothes Mentor

Buffalo Exchange

Collectibles

Almost anything can be a collectible. When someone takes a serious interest and develops a zest for a topic, movie series, animal, etc. – they can end up creating a collection of items related to the topic of their interest, therefore becoming a collector of collectible items.

For example, I love elephants. They are the largest land mammal alive now and are generally gentle, loving, family-oriented, emotional, intelligent animals that I admire greatly. I have elephant pants, jewelry, candleholders, a cake pan, elephant paintings my artist daughter has created, elephant journals, etc. I illustrate this point to show that because I have an interest and love for them, I myself collect these items, and the people around me get them for me as gifts.

So, what do you collect? And more importantly, is it something you want to part with? My elephant collection is only valuable to me, and I would not part with it.

For some, it is a collectible that has been passed on to them that they have no interest in holding onto or adding to. For some, it will be a matter of having such an urgent need for the funds that it will generate that they have to be willing to let it go.

The most popular collectibles, and therefore the collectibles with the largest markets, are antique furniture, vinyl records, comic books, coins and currency, classic cars, trading cards, dolls and toys, stamps, wine, and fine art and jewelry.

There are other more modern collectible items such as action figures, board games, star wars items, movie items, certain toys, sports memorabilia, watches, music paraphernalia, movie posters, medals and badges, video games, and Legos, to name a few.

Although the items listed above are what is most common, your own collection of collectibles has some worth, and a buyer looking for what you have.

As is the case with everything you sell, you will need to arm yourself with information before you begin your selling process so that you can get the best results.

First, know your item or set of items' worth. In order to make that evaluation, it is very helpful to know what similar items are selling for currently. The current part is an important variable because collectible items tend to fluctuate with the market, trends, and demands at the time you are selling.

Once you have found the comparable selling prices of similar items, you must look at the condition of your item compared to that of the item sold.

The rarity of the collectible naturally lends to the deciding factor in how much you can possibly expect to get for your collectible.

Lastly, how and where you sell your item will play a huge

role in the amount of money you can expect to make. For example, if someone has an urgent need and has to take their items to a pawn shop, they will have to expect a great deal less than if they are able to invest time and resources into listing it with an appropriate, specific selling source that will bring more money but will take far more time.

Where to sell your collectibles online:

Neatstuff Collectibles - https://neatstuffcollectibles.com/

Heritage Auctions - https://www.ha.com/how-to-sell-my-collection.s?ic=Tab-ToSell-040814

Morphy's Auctions - https://www.morphyauctions.com/consigning/

Skinner Auctions - https://www.skinnerinc.com/auctions/

Keno Auctions - https://www.kenoauctions.com/selling/

Neatstuff Collectibles – There are no details on exactly how their selling process works. The only specific information they offer is what they do and do not want to buy. Other than that, you are directed to a form to complete or a phone number to call, 1-800-326-7064, to discuss what can be done.

Items they DO want Star Wars collectibles, Nintendo and other video games, collectible toys, art, memorabilia – sports, music, and movies, and more.

Items they do NOT want include furniture, fine art, VHS/CDs/DVDs, happy meal toys, beanie babies, NASCAR, Hess trucks, and other diecast cars

Heritage Auctions - Wow. As simple as the site described above is, this one is that much detail-oriented, information-packed, and takes some time to navigate. While this site is being listed in the collectibles section, it can also be used for other categories, such as jewelry, art, and antiques. This powerhouse of an entity has been around since 1976, serving over 200,000 consignors in a number of ways spanning a spectrum of items.

There are three ways to consign with Heritage – free auction evaluation, outright sell, or ask an expert.

Heritage offers a free auction evaluation that is initiated by filling out a form detailing your collection and including photos. Additionally, there are also many tools on this site to educate oneself about their items. There are value guides grouped by category that walk you through the process of evaluating your item(s). There is a link to auction archives to see what similar items have sold for previously. The grading tutorial again is grouped by category and then goes on to explain how each collectible type is graded, which leads to its ultimate appraisal. I could have spent days on this site just soaking myself in the world that apparently is collectibles, auctions, and all of the processes those contain.

The outright sell option is the same; you are led to a form to fill out with your item description and photographs, and then an appraisal is given. The site states that there are generous cash advances available for large amounts of material.

Lastly, they ask for an expert option – the same process,

fill out the online form with item details, including photographs, and wait for a response.

If you do not take the outright sell option, your collectible items are going to auction. If you have the ability to wait on your money, auctions are historically the way to achieve the most funds.

The auction process in a nutshell:

Your items make their way to Heritage, and you are notified by the consignment director, who will also be your primary contact through this process.

The consignment director inspects and identifies your items using your name and client data.

Graders will determine the appropriate auction venues for your goods and evaluate what items may need to be certified or resubmitted.

Your confidential consignment is available at My Consignments.

The items are professionally described with photographs to match and prepared for the website.

Website bidding begins, and registered bidder-members can begin to bid for several weeks.

The big day of the actual auction arrives, and bidders all compete in bidding on your collection.

Your settlement check is mailed to you 45 days after the auction has closed.

Morphy's Auctions – This auction house specializes in seven divisions of auction materials: advertising and general store, automobilia and petroliana, coin-op and gambling, fine and decorative arts, firearms, toys, and pop culture and the site states that they are "specializing in fresh to the market collections." This phrase means that the collections they focus on have been amassed over a 30+ year period and are fresh to the auction marketplace.

In order to start the consignment process, a Morphy Auctions representative has to evaluate your materials. There are three ways to contact them: a) contact by phone, 877-968-8880, b) send photos by email info@morphyauctions.com, or c) fill out the online consignment form.

The auction process takes 5-6 months to allow proper time to market, advertise, and create catalogs.

There are about 25-30 auctions held per year, and payment is issued on or before the 45th day following the auction.

Skinner Auctions – Skinner's has expertise in dozens of specialty areas, allowing them to appraise and auction items of value from every culture and time period.

This broad spectrum of connoisseurship also enables Skinner to sell items singly, as part of a large collection, or as an institutional collection.

For the purposes of this text, the steps to begin the single item assessment will be covered. Seeing is believing, and visuals are crucial when trying to determine if a consignment can be accepted.

A consignor can submit images for an auction evaluation online, send photographs by mail, or set up an appointment with an appraiser.

After the material is reviewed and accepted on consignment, the auction process will begin.

Skinner's auction process:

Consigned material will need to make its way to one of the galleries, with a detailed packing list.

The consignment contract is issued with details on auction estimates, auction processes, and commission rates and fees.

Over a 2-3 month time period, there will be a massive undertaking of photography, marketing, outreach, and catalog production.

Two weeks before the auction, a pre-sale notice will be sent out.

Auction attendance can happen in person at the gallery or online using Skinnerlive.

Sold! The payment the consignor receives is based on the hammer price, and you can expect to receive payment 35 days after the auction.

Keno Auctions - https://www.kenoauctions.com/selling/

Where to sell collectibles offline:

Garage/yard sales

Pawnshops

Auction house

Flea market

Collectible dealers (coins, stamps, comic books, etc.)

Crafting Supplies

Pretty much anything that can be purchased at a craft store can be sold elsewhere too. This can include things like beads, buttons, fabric, yarn, paints, artist canvas, silk flowers, rubber stamps, ribbons, pens and markers, scrapbooking supplies, and the tools needed to create crafts. Those tools can include things self-healing mats, X-acto knives, glue guns, needle-nose pliers, Dremels, wood-burning implements, metal snips, scissors of all kinds, paper trimmer, and a whole slew of other gadgets.

The crafting materials themselves need to be pretty much brand new or so gently used that there is no visible wear. The tools can have a little more use as long as they are still in great condition and perform their task perfectly. No one wants tiny pom poms that are misshapen from having been cut off a previous craft project, but they will be willing to buy those thirty-dollar scissors you only used three times.

My mom is a moderate craft enthusiast and has managed to amass almost a whole room full of crafting supplies. While she does not have a monetary need as a reason to pare down on some of her crafting supplies, she does need her space back. Those extra 10 spools of purple fabric from my brother's wedding two years ago could definitely free up some space.

For some people, the issue may be more about freeing up some space at home rather than making a little cash.

Either way, you will most likely find the best results using a website where you can sell almost anything, such as Facebook, Craigslist, eBay, or Etsy.

Where to sell craft supplies online:

Facebook marketplace and groups

Craigslist

eBay

Etsy

Shopify

Where to sell craft supplies offline:

Garage/yard sale

Flea market

Craft convention

Décor

Home décor is all the decorative pieces that adorn the inside of a home. No matter how minimal your decorative style, if you look around, you will probably see some sort of home décor items.

These items can include wall accents, mirrors, paintings, clocks, candles, vases, urns, figurines, decorative bowls, trays, bottles, and the list can continue and on. Personally, I prefer something that serves multiple purposes. I love, love, love the ottomans that have the storage compartments inside. Or the decorative wall piece that is a mirror and small shelf in one.

Home décor adds personality and comfort to our homes. Sometimes we are gifted a piece of décor that just doesn't vibe with our current theme or, on our own, we decide to change the flavor of the room.

Fetch some bucks with pieces of home décor you can part with. I myself live in a tiny space, so the really cool three wall clock, oversized painting, and collection of decorative candle holders are welcome to go when the time goes. These items will bring a few more drops to the bucket and clear up some space in my storage trailer.

When you are taking pictures for your online posts and ads, try to photograph the item where it would normally be in a living space – hung on the wall, rug on the floor, throw pillow on the couch, candle, and holder on an end table. This will help your prospective buyer envision it in their space.

If and when you can, offer to group items together as a set and offer it at a slightly lower price. The buyer can enjoy a discount, and you will get the advantage of selling more items at one time rather than multiple times.

This is one of those categories that do not have a lot of specialty sites, so make sure to make the most of the sell-almost-anything platforms such as Mercari, Facebook marketplace, and groups, eBay, craigslist.

Where to sell your décor online:

Apartment Therapy Bazaar - https://marketplace.apartmenttherapy.com/

Chairish - https://www.chairish.com/

Everything but the house (EBTH) - https://www.ebth.com/

Apartment Therapy Bazaar – This easy to use site is "a community-driven marketplace for vintage designer furnishings and accessories."

The mission statement of the company is slightly vague. But when you delve into the FAQ's, the specificity of their items and the demographics they are trying to reach becomes clear.

In their words, listings that are considered "high-quality designer, vintage, antique, and secondhand" are welcomed. Their listing feed is centered on these categories: furniture, accessories, lighting, tabletop, and rugs, with subcategories for each. Even the market they target has been narrowed down to luxe (high quality, classic, rare), style grade (new and vintage pieces, great brands and designers), and everyday (mass-market brands for basic collections).

This is how it works: 1) Fill out your store profile to join the community. 2) Click SELL to publish your first listing. 3) Set up stripe payments to be able to accept electronic payments. (This is optional. If you would rather use a 3rd party payment processor like PayPal, that is an option. Buyers would message the seller directly for payment) 4) Accept or reject the order and be sure to include any shipping/delivery fees. The seller will not be prompted to begin the delivery process until the order has been paid in full. 5) You can mark the order as complete after you have finalized the shipping/delivery process.

There is no membership to enroll in, and the only fees the seller incurs are when an item sells. The service fee that is paid to the site is 5.9% + $00.30.

In order to be able to access your earnings, you will have to create a stripe account. Your personal and/or business information will be required to complete the process and become a certified seller. The Stripe dashboard is where you will see all of your earning information as it becomes available. You can either use Stripe to collect funds or link another payment processor.

Chairish – Chairish aims to be the go-to shop for "exceptional home furnishings and art." Three core themes drive this definition of exceptionalism – curation, full service, and trust. Every item listed here is examined by professional curators to ensure all materials meet their high standards. Chairish takes the stress off both the buyer and seller by facilitating the shipping from the seller to the buyer. To establish trust and consistency, the site allows shoppers two days to communicate that they want to return an item. Sellers are not paid until this window has passed, which helps maintain a marginal return rate and a higher degree of trust and efficiency.

Chairish's selling process is designed to create and

maintain satisfaction for both the buyer and the seller.

All listings are free, all items are curated to ensure quality, only verified buyers and sellers can utilize the site, Chairish organizes shipping, and sellers are paid via PayPal as soon as the 48-hour return window has passed.

There are four selling plans to choose from consignor, professional, elite, and warehouse.

Consignor status allows the seller to post 1-9 active listings, and a 30% flat rate commission is deducted from all sales, and there are no membership fees.

The professional plan is also a free membership, with 10+ active listings.

Everything but the house (EBTH) – The full description for this site is listed under antiques but is also a great platform to use for selling décor items.

Where to sell your décor offline:

Garage/yard sale

Flea market

Community sale

Electronics

We now live in a world of electronics. I try to limit my use of them for many conspiracy theory related reasons, but the truth is that we cannot function without them.

Even though I attempt to limit my electronic footprint and interaction, the truth is that I sit at home right now, typing on a laptop that is hooked up to a router, with my cell phone on the table beside me while a smart tv provides some background entertainment via Wi-Fi and a firestick.

Except for the laptop, all of the abovementioned items are of mediocre quality and more than likely more than a little outdated.

Well, once the pandemic reared its ugly head, and then a slew of other phenomena continued to affect our daily lives, causing people to become more prone to stay inside of their own homes, their personal electronics usage became more prevalent. Whether they had transitioned to working from home and now had to use the necessities to perform their job or were using other electronics for entertainment and convenience.

Everything can be automated now. Alexa can read a recipe out loud to you, your smart fridge can remind you that you need to get milk soon, and we all stay connected with our smartphones.

Technology continues to change and evolve, which means that there is always the latest and greatest new device.

Many people like me are content with last year's model if it still functions. Collate some cash by getting rid of electronics that are not at the top of your have to have a list or that you have already upgraded.

With electronics, there is a specialized set of rules/tips to adhere to:

Sell early – Since tech products decrease in value almost immediately, you want to get rid of your item as soon as you make the decision that it is no longer needed. The longer you hold onto it, the more the value decreases.

Protect your privacy – Very important, make sure that you perform a factory reset on any device you are parting with so that none of your personal information leaves with the electronic item. My browsing history and pictures (while mostly innocent) are no one else's business. And most importantly, you have to safeguard any banking information you might have saved.

Pictures make a difference – This is always important with anything you sell. It helps to set your item against a solid colored background.

Complete transparency – Tell the whole truth about your item. Is there a small nick or scratch on the edge of your tablet that you can't see in the picture? Mention it in your ad. It will bother some people when they receive it without knowing about it beforehand and will lend to your credibility.

Because of the amount of electronics in our world today, there is a plethora of places to list your item online.

If one site does not take your device, there may be another a little less particular; see the next section of the text for details on the details for each site.

Where to sell your electronics online:

Decluttr - https://www.decluttr.com/start-selling/

Gazelle - https://www.gazelle.com/

BuybackBoss - https://buybackboss.com/

Nextworth - https://www.nextworth.com/

Trademore - https://www.trademore.com/

ecoATM - https://www.ecoatm.com/

Swappa - https://swappa.com/

Sellshark - https://sellshark.com/

Buybackworld - https://www.buybackworld.com/

Gazelle - This is a site where you can sell phones and electronics, specifically iPhones, Samsung phones, Google phones, iPad, MacBooks, and iPods. The 3-step process is meant to be easy and relatively fast:

1) you can get an offer in less than a minute

2) when the item is worth more than $1, you get to ship it for free

3) receive fast payment with either a check, PayPal, or Amazon gift card

BuybackBoss – Like gazelle, this site also offers a simple three-step selling system when you get a quick offer, use free shipping, and then paid by PayPal or check. One difference between the two is that this site seems to buy a larger variety of electronics items, including laptops, computers, camcorders, game systems, and a variety of other items.

Nextworth - Again, this platform promises an easy selling solution for phones and electronics. Get quoted, ship the item for free, and then get paid via PayPal or check. The site states that they are currently accepting smartphones, tablets, and wearables. In the FAQ pages, it explains that the quote for your item is determined by its condition, configuration, and current secondary market value. The quote is good for 30 days from the date it is made.

Trademore – Another electronics buyback program, this one works similar to the others listed above. You get paid with either a virtual MasterCard or through PayPal, and payment is typically processed within 5 business days from the date of receiving your device.

ecoATM – The ecoAtm is an in-person option. You take your phone, fully charged, with a valid identification card to one of the available kiosks, plug in your device so that the ecoATM can read your device, evaluate its worth, and then get paid cash on the spot.

Swappa – Swappa buys iPhones, other smartphones, phone plans, laptops, watches, and tablets. The process for this platform is more like a traditional online marketplace. Here, you will search for your item to see other devices like it to compare pricing, then you create a listing for swappa users to see, and once your item is sold, you are paid instantly via PayPal even before the item has shipped. Because you are creating a selling ad on the site and connecting with a buyer, you also have the option of selling in person.

Buybackworld – Similar to some of the other sites detailed above, here you will sell your item by getting a quote, then shipping it out for free, and get paid within two days of the receipt of your item by either check, PayPal, direct deposit, a buybackworld.com gift card, or a prepaid debit card. This site buys almost everything electronic, including phones, iPad, MacBooks, desktops, accessories, gaming equipment, cameras, and smartwatches.

Where to sell electronics offline:

You probably want to try to limit your electronic sales to online interactions. You can definitely use whatever platform you choose to find your buyer and then arrange to meet in person, but chances are that you will not have good results trying to sell your items at a typical person-to-person selling avenue.

Furniture

Here's a quick story and a lesson learned that I want to share with you. I was recently helping my mom sell some of her excess stuff, including a set of living room tables, because she was changing out her living room furniture.

Well, we did really well in the sense that we took measurements, took good pictures, and used great descriptors, and then had multiple people interested in the items when we were selling on the Facebook marketplace.

An epic fail occurred when we preloaded the pieces in the back of her truck, which has a camper on it. They were left in there for 48 hours in the south Texas summertime heat, and when we opened the back to sell them, the "wood" had swollen, and the glue holding the metal legs and the "wood" together had melted and come undone. Needless to say, the tables were ruined.

Lesson learned. Store the furniture you are going to sell right up until the sale day and time in the same environment it is going to be housed in.

With that being said, here are some key points to keep in mind when you decide to sell any of your used furniture:

Assess the condition – And keep it in that state until you can get it to your buyer. See the valuable lesson learned above.

Take timing into consideration – Furniture market trends are similar to real estate trends. So, it seems likely that it will sell quickly at the beginning of the month when people are moving into new places and during the summer when people move into new homes.

Taking timing one step further, we are in the middle of a pandemic, and there are plenty of people who are justifiably worried about bringing germs into their house. Take the time to disinfect your pieces thoroughly, and make sure to mention it in your ad.

Measurements matter – Carefully measure all of the

dimensions of the item so that your buyer will know if it will fit in their home before they take it home. Include any details like storage or hidden compartments.

Five photos minimum – Pictures at different angles and views will help give your buying audience a better idea of what they are contemplating buying.

Why are you selling – Include your reasons for why you are letting go of your furniture. Did you change up your living room vibe, downsize, or have a baby? Whatever the reason, include it in your ad. It seems to help people understand why you are selling and motivates the right buyer.

There are some things that I prefer to sell person to person. Furniture is one of them. If it were a second hand, hand me down, I would only sell it at some sort of garage/yard sale or at a flea market type situation.

If it were a newer and/or higher quality item, I would take the time to get all the measurements, take great pictures and then create an online post, find my buyer, and then meet with them in person.

I would utilize one of the sites where you can sell almost anything and go from there.

However, everyone is different, and so are their unique needs, resources, skills, and situations, so there a few furniture specific online selling options listed below.

If I were selling an item that was of higher quality, brand name, and very gently used, I would utilize the option that brought me the most return.

Where to sell your furniture online:

Chairish - https://www.chairish.com/

Sotheby's - https://sell.sothebyshome.com/

Apartment Therapy Bazaar - https://marketplace.apartmenttherapy.com/

Ruby Lane - https://www.rubylane.com/info/lanereqs

Where to sell your furniture offline:

Antique store

Consignment shop

Used furniture store

Garage/yard sale

Community sale

Estate sale

Local newspaper

Gift Cards

I have made money in lots of ways and sometimes been paid in unorthodox ways. One time, I answered a Craigslist post for a very deep cleaning of an apartment with a woman who had two cats and some mental health issues.

The place was awful, and I do mean terrible. The reason I

include this here is that, in addition to paying me the agreed-upon sum, she also included a very thick stack of gift cards to all kinds of businesses that had various amounts on them. Some were virtual credit cards and could be used pretty much anywhere. Some of the other cards were to places I really don't frequent and was better off selling them for cash, even if it meant taking a small loss on the total sum. For example, I had an Express card that had roughly $75 on it. After fees and discounts, I ended up netting about $60 in cash.

So, however you ended up with a handful of gift cards, there are ways to sell them. Of course, you won't get the total amount that the card was purchased for, but that should be expected.

There are some instances where you can sell these in person, but unless you are able to find someone easily through a group or a sell-almost-anything site, I would definitely recommend utilizing a specialty site. The specialty site will take care of everything. You supply all the information, card number, balance, asking price, etc.; the site verifies the information, gets you a buyer, and issues your payment via the method of your choice.

Where to sell your gift cards online:

Raise - https://www.raise.com/sell-gift-cards

Cardpool - https://sell.cardpool.com/

CardCash - https://www.cardcash.com/sell-gift-cards

ClipKard - https://www.clipkard.com/

Gift Card Granny - https://www.giftcardgranny.com/sell-a-gift-card/

GC Spread - https://www.giftcardspread.com/sell-gift-cards

Raise – Here, you will be able to sell gift cards and store credits for funds that you can use anywhere. You will need to locate your gift card, create a listing for it, and then once it is sold, you get paid with either direct deposit, PayPal, or check. Gift cards and store credits are accepted from most brands, retailers, and restaurants. Physical cards must have a minimum balance of $10, ecards minimum of $5, and the value must be under $2,000.

Cardpool – This site is different than raise because you are not creating a listing. Instead, you enter the card information, get a payout quote of up to 88% of the card's value, and currently, the only way to receive payment is via an ACH deposit into your bank account.

CardCash – Similar structure as others,

1) Select offer; really, you just type in the name of the merchant (Target, Starbucks, etc.) with the total amount and get an instant quote. I typed in a $100 value for Target and was offered $68

2) Submit your cards – enter the card number and pin

3) Get verified and paid. Payment methods are check mailed to you, ACH payment, or PayPal

You also have the option of trading your card for 9% more if you select a different gift card. Payment is issued after a balance and fraud check is performed. Payout is typically issued 24-48 hours after order approval.

ClipKard – Same thing, you give the business name, the amount, get a quote, and ultimately get paid. The biggest difference here is that you are required to ship your card in. Payout methods are either by check in the mail and takes 5-14 days or with PayPal and the payment can take up to 3 days to post to the account. The payment process is initiated once the shipping of the cards has been verified and takes 3-10 business days to post to your account.

Where to sell offline:

Unless you happen to have personal connections with people that you know are interested in buying your gift cards, it is probably best to stick to online arrangements.

Housewares

The term housewares seems to have a few meanings and cross through different categories.

If you type housewares into your search bar, there will be one site that refers to housewares in a more decorative sense. Another will be referencing housewares as small appliances and gadgets.

For the most part, the consensus seems to be that housewares can be used to describe all of the smaller items that help to make a house a home.

These items can range from kitchen items like pots and pans (though I would call those dishes), small appliances like coffee pots, mixers, blenders, etc., to include all of the tools and utensils.

In the dining room, housewares can be items like placemats, napkin rings, glassware, china, and even serving platters and bowls.

Moving further into the house, all of the bathroom items can be things like the essentials – washcloths, hand towels, shower caddies, soap dishes, and even the shower curtain itself. There are even small bathroom appliances you might consider, such as digital scales and waterproof radios.

In your bedroom areas, things like shoe racks, shelves, and stacking containers are utilitarian items that can be considered housewares and not be bedding or ornamental.

All of the usual rules apply as far as taking good pictures, choosing your selling option, and being a clear and concise communicator.

Additionally, because a lot of housewares can be smaller items, try to sell them as sets whenever you can.

I would say that you will have equal success, depending on your location, resources, and availability when it comes to choosing to sell your houseware items either on or offline.

For the online options, utilize any of the sell-almost-anything sites.

If you are going to sell these items offline, be sure, and have enough combined items to sell in an organized sale such as a garage sale or at a flea market.

Jewelry

I do hope that this text is able to reach as diverse an audience as possible because diversity, our differences is what makes us all so unique and interesting. There is no one like me. There is no one like you—all the way down the building blocks of our very beings, our DNA.

Jewelry can be as wide-ranging in worth, types, and reasons for wearing it as the people who do.

I, myself, have always been a simple soul. And if/when I become rich, there a few things I will completely go all out on when it comes to materialistic things. Jewelry is one of them.

I don't know about men, but for girls and women, jewelry can be very important. Whether you are just wearing a simple friendship bracelet made from embroidery thread or you're *blingin'* enough ice to warrant hiring a bodyguard crew, most of us have at least some small love for jewelry.

Now, the friendship bracelet you've had since the eighth

grade is only worth the sentimental value you attach to it. But almost everything in between on the spectrum of plastic bangles to diamond-encrusted tiaras will sell.

Naturally, jewelry with precious metals and stones will fetch the highest price because the value is not only in the artistry or the current trend but is also in the actual material of the item(s).

Antique and collectors' pieces are specialty markets whose trends fluctuate with the market. For example, pre-coronavirus, when people had less fear and a more steady income. Now, in August 2020, as we continue to live through a chapter in history, that value has had to change. So, the prices you would have seen for your grandmother's brooch in November 2019 may not be the same that you do today.

One study that examined the impact that the pandemic has had on the U.S. retail economy reports that "US specialty jewelry retailers saw their sales drop some 82% in the span of just two months … [and] sales of $2.65 billion … dropped to … $470 million in April". (edahngolan.com)

These ginormous numbers are not meant to shock you or further disturb you more than you already might be. If you are reading this, you may be someone who would never have had to sell their things before, and now, as a result of the coronavirus, your life has drastically changed. I feel for you, feeling like you have no control and the security you once knew is shattered.

I grew up upper lower class, have a very complicated, crazy backstory, and am no stranger to hardships and limited resources for long periods of time. Anyhow, the point is, I am sorry for you if this is how this has affected you. Good news for you though, you are sitting on a mini gold mine.

In addition to buying trends having plummeted, the market is also saturated with other buyers also needing to save themselves and their families.

These sobering statements are here to help soften the blow when you get an estimate, quote, or offer on your beautiful piece, and it is far lower than you would have ever thought. If you can wait to sell it, that would be my best advice to you. When life gets closer to normal, whenever that might be, then there will be another trend where the demand is higher and the suppliers not so urgent and desperate.

So, what do you have?

Earrings, bracelets, necklaces, rings, maybe a brooch? Do you have a tie pin set that you inherited? My sister had a "costume" piece, a tiara, for her quinceanera/sweet sixteen that was purchased for over two hundred dollars. Do you have something cool and rare? Do you have high-quality hand-made pieces created by a designer with a following? Is your mouthpiece gleaming with "the whole top diamond and the bottom row gold"?

After you decide whether or not you are going to sell it here and now, take the next step of accepting that you will take a loss. Making peace with it before selling it is crucial. Lastly, before selling your jewelry, determine how much time you have. There is a buyer for almost anything at the price you want, but when? Anyone willing/able to wait will always have a higher chance of getting what they want for their items.

Narrow down your jewelry to its category so that you can sell to the audience that wants what you have, netting you the most cash.

Gold and precious metals/stones – Whether you are selling your gold for fast cash to a gold buyer or taking your time and selling it piece by piece as jewelry, arm yourself with information.

When it comes time for the buyer to make their offer and then negotiate, you have a selling advantage when you know your items' worth.

Today, August 18, 2020, the price of gold is $65.43 per gram and $2,035.00 per ounce. (monex.com)

If your pieces are not on the high end or you need to get as much money as soon as possible, you can go to a gold buyer, where they buy by the weight.

Express gold cash - https://www.expressgoldcash.com/faqs/

Cash for gold USA - https://cashforgoldusa.com/

Sell your gold - https://www.sellyourgold.com/

These are all online gold buyers with very similar, simple buying processes. Basically, you contact them, request some sort of appraisal kit, ship your items back to them in the packaging they included in the kit, they make an offer, and you get paid – usually very quickly too.

This option is great for people who need fast, simple funds and would rather do it all from the comfort of home.

If you want to go in person, look up your local gold buyer, pawnshop, or jewelry.

On the other hand, if you have high-value pieces and/or pieces that also have stones in them, you may want to consider taking the route that takes more time and effort if your situation allows you to.

With the higher dollar items, you will want to get a current appraisal first. An insurance jewelry appraisal should cost roughly $50-$150. The price will depend on the complexity, rarity, and what establishment you end up using. This investment helps you know what to expect and what to charge.

The following are reputable, accredited appraisers who can act solely as a third party, ensuring that the appraisal is accurate:

American Gem Society - https://www.americangemsociety.org/search/custom.asp?id=4711

National Association of Jewelry Appraisers –

http://www.najaappraisers.com/html/find_an_appraiser.php

Gemological Institute of America –

https://www.gia.edu/gia-faq

In addition to providing your appraisal, these organizations have the professional experience and knowledge to guide you to a specific buyer, site, or selling platform.

After you get the appraisal and direction about where your piece(s) will sell best, do some research and then narrow down your options.

When you are selling gold in person, the same options are available – gold buying entities who buy for weight and can be found with a local search, pawnshops, local jewelers, auctions, jewelry parties, antique and collectible dealers, and one-to-one exchanges.

Three things to remember – 1) find its value, 2) educate yourself on the current market, and 3) research your appraiser and buyer.

Antique and collectible jewelry – All of the same basic rules apply to selling antique and collectible jewelry as they do for gold and stones. You will need to know how much it is currently valued at, the most recent trend, and do your due diligence to find the appraiser and buyer.

A lot of antique and collectible pieces will be made of precious metals and stones, so you still want to know the current value of the medium itself. Because age and rarity are the driving factors, you will need to target buyers who specialize in those fields specifically.

Listed below are buyers whose specialization and sole focus is in antique and collectible jewelry:

Luriya - https://www.luriya.com/page/sell-antique-jewelry

Worthy - https://vip.worthy.com/lp/sell-jewelry

Scott Gram Antiques - https://scottgramantiques.com/faq/

Handmade and Costume Jewelry – When selling handmade and costume jewelry, the deciding factors should be how much of the jewelry you have to sell and how much time and effort you can put into the sale.

For a quicker fix, use the sell-almost-anything sites like Etsy, eBay, Facebook marketplace and groups, craigslist, offerup and similar platforms.

If you have a large inventory and/or higher-quality pieces,

you may want to explore the sites that specialize in handmade pieces. People who are using these sites are already specifically seeking out unique handmade and costume pieces, so they are more likely to pay more for that special item that catches their fancy.

Check out these sites:

Aftcra - https://www.aftcra.com/become-a-seller

Art Fire - https://www.artfire.com/ext/sell/start_today

Shop Handmade - http://www.shophandmade.com/Tour#Selling

Rebels Market - https://www.rebelsmarket.com/seller_applications/new

Express gold cash –

1) request an appraisal kit to be mailed to you for free, or you can download the label to expedite the process

2) After you send your gold in at an authorized local FedEx: a. confirmation sent once the gold kit is received and b. verification is done to confirm that the items match the inventory list, and c. An offer is calculated using the type of material, weight, and the daily price of gold

3) Once the offer is accepted, payment is issued within 24 hours. If you decline the offer, the items are sent back immediately, for free, with no questions asked.

Cash for gold USA – This site focuses on gold but also accepts silver, platinum, and palladium. It also offers some helpful information on testing your pieces at home to determine if they are real, how to predict your estimate, and other useful tips. The process is almost exactly the same, but this one, you use an online form to request a SAFEPAK, send it in, email with an offer within 24 hours of receipt, and payment made upon acceptance of the offer.

Sellyourgold – While this site follows the same process with a couple of interesting differences. In the shipping packet sent to mail your items in, there is a 5% bonus card that you can send in with your items for some more cash. The other big difference is that the other sites insure up to $5,000 while sellyourgold provides a $100,000 insurance on your items.

For finer items with higher payout making it worth the wait:

Worthy – The three-step process:

1) pickup by FedEx

2) they do all the work

3) how you get paid is a little more complicated than the ones listed above. Before beginning the process of mailing in your items, you will be asked to describe your value to assess if this is the right path for both parties. Then, you will need to send your pieces in for authentication. You can schedule a pick-up time or drop it off with FedEx.

The reason they say they do all the work is that this is not a weight of value method for payment. With this site, your valuables will be placed for sale at an auction. Once received, your item(s) are screened to verify that they meet auction eligibility. Upon approval, the real work starts. a) the pieces are cleaned to remove any dirt or tarnish, b) professional pictures are taken, c) grading is performed by a gemologist or an industry-leading lab, d) an auction listing is created, e) you set your reserve price, which the lowest amount you want your valuable sold for, f) the auction begins, and then you are paid.

Payment is either your reserve price or the highest bid at the auction. There is a commission deducted from the sale price, 18% for sales up to $5,000, 14% for $5,000-$15,000, 12% for $15,000-$30,000, and anything more than that is 10%.

Payout is issued via PayPal in 1-2 business days, bank transfer in 2-3 business days, or by check-in 4-5 business days.

If you have a collection of homemade, artisan, boutique jewelry – basically jewelry that has value in its uniqueness, artistry, creators' portfolio, and other reasons. The value in these works is in the design and meaning with less emphasis on the stone and the metal.

Artfire – Here, you can sell all items that are handmade, vintage, and craft supplies. With this platform, you will have to set up a 'shop' with a choice of three levels – standard: $4.95 per month with a $00.23 per item listing fee, 12.75% final valuation fee; popular: $20.00 per month and 4.5% final valuation fee with up to 1000 active listings, or the featured shop which is $40.00 per month and 4.5% final valuation fee and allowed up to 2500 active listing. For each level, there are additional features.

This option is good for those who have a very large inventory or other items they can use to make up their shops, such as vintage and craft items.

Aftcra – This site is specifically designed for handmade or handcrafted items only, including jewelry, clothing, kids and baby, home and furnishings, arts and handicrafts, celebration items such as bridal pieces, and other occasion-specific items, paper goods, and accessories.

The central focus of this site is to only sell items that are handcrafted by people living and producing these items in the USA.

To be able to set up a shop and sell with aftcra, the items must be: "handcrafted or handmade... upcycled or repurposed... [or] prints, photographs, digital prints, and screen-printed goods."

These types of items are NOT allowed to be sold on this site: "products not handcrafted in the USA... vintage goods... manufactured products... reselling of products that are not created by the shop owner... and blatant copyright infringement".

All sellers can set up a shop and list their items for free, and all listings stay active for 6 months and, if need be, can be relisted for another 6 months for free when the initial time expires. The only fee that is deducted by aftcra is 7% of the sale fee.

Kids' Stuff

My sister has four boys ages seven to sixteen and always manages to keep them looking super stylish with quality name brand clothes, some of the newest toys, and tech stuff and regularly updates their bedrooms and furnishings.

And she does this on a moderate budget. She does this by buying a savvy shopper, keeping track of sales, discounts, and coupons, and buying used anytime she can.

You would never know it to look at them, their play items, or their rooms, that the majority of it was preowned.

In her case, she has four boys, so she can also cycle different pieces that have life left in them from the older to the younger.

When something doesn't fit, the new owner of the hand-me-down doesn't need or want the item, or they are just making some upgrades, she then resells those items.

The two biggest kids' items sellers are clothes and shoes. These are their two biggest necessities and the two things they are always growing out of.

Any site that buys and sells kids' clothing and shoes is only going to buy quality items because that's all most people will buy.

Try these online buying and selling options:

Kidizen - https://kidizen.com/seller-handbook/

Children's Orchard - https://www.childrensorchard.com/sell/

Kid to Kid - https://kidtokid.com/how-it-works/how-to-sell/

In addition to allowing you to buy and sell clothes and shoes, there also listings for toys, accessories, and furnishings.

For anything electronic or tech-related: games, phones, interactive toys, drones, etc., see the section on electronics.

When it comes to toys, in addition to the sell-almost-anything platforms, there are a few specialty sites that focus on toys.

Fiddle Piddle - https://fiddlepiddle.com/how-to-sell/

B 2 B Kids Resale - https://b2bkidsresale.com/sell/

As far as kids' furnishings, outdoor and sports equipment, musical instruments, and others, check the other sections that directly pertain to those categories.

Kidizen - This platform sells items for babies, little girls and boys, and everything for mama, including clothes, shoes, and accessories.

There are two ways to sell your items here – create and manage your own listings, or use a 'style scout,' a personal seller that will do all of the work for you.

If you choose the independent route, you will click on create listing and then be prompted to register with an email address, name, and password, and then you are immediately taken to a listing screen to attach photos and fill in all the details on what you have.

For every sale, kidizen gets 12% plus a $00.50 fee on all transactions. This is a very simple explanation of the per listing fee taken from the total sale.

After an item is sold, the next step is to purchase a shipping label and then provide a tracking number within

7 days of the purchase date.

Finally, the funds due to the seller are transferred from 'pending kid bucks' to 'redeemable kid bucks.' After the monies are in the redeemable stage, the seller can then use them to make purchases on kidizen or have the funds cashed out to a PayPal or bank account.

The other option is to utilize a 'style scout' who will consult with you, remotely or in-person with a house call to assess what top-selling, high-quality items you have for mama and the crew.

When using this route, the scout takes over the entire process, including: "free in-home consultation... listing [and] photographing the items... management and promotion of listings... [and] shipping once the items sell.

Using a style scout will cost half of the profits after fees and shipping are deducted.

This is a great site for those mamas with an excess of quality items for themselves and their little people. Adding to its appeal is the fact that it is the only online site devoted only to mama, baby, and little ones.

The other options are the sell almost anything sites and to sell items in person at local stores.

Musical Instruments

Oh, the joy of music. Seriously, music has serious effects on all aspects of our health and wellbeing. Listening to and participating in making music has been known to help reduce stress, lower blood pressure, and improve cognitive performance, to name a few.

Music moves us in many ways and has been a part of society and culture since ancient times. That means longevity in the selling market.

When I was a preteen, moving into my teen years, I played the flute. Not because I had any natural passion for playing a classical instrument, but because I was a nerd and was looking for a group of people who would accept me through a common interest.

Little did I know that I had some inherent ability to read and follow along to sheet music, but I apparently also had lips that were perfectly shaped for the embouchure of the flute, meaning that the sound I created came effortlessly.

While my flute playing career did take me to some UIL competitions with my newfound friends and help me develop another part of myself, it was also short-lived.

After two short but successful years of being in a band, I was suddenly too cool and, honestly, too lost in what was going on to focus on the success I could have made with it or really enjoy the experience.

I digress. That flute, along with my brother's saxophone, my sister's clarinet, my mom's old piano, and the drum set my ex-husband left behind all had long lives with their original owners and then were sold to others for their next journey.

Use these resources to find the value of your instrument, compare prices on other similar items, and sell your pieces:

Reverb - https://reverb.com/

Music Go Round - https://www.musicgoround.com/home/sell-us-your-gear

Sam Ash Music Store - https://used.samashmusic.com/want-used-gear/

Rogue Music Store - https://www.roguemusic.com/selling.html

Reverb – Just like its name implies, this is a site to buy and sell musical instruments. There is a focus on guitars, pedals and amplifiers, keyboards and synths, recording gear, drums, and DJ and audio gear.

In the 'more categories' drop-down menu, there are subcategories for band and orchestra pieces (flutes, violins, saxophones), folk instruments like banjos and ukuleles, and you will also see software.

It is free to create your listing. The fees are only deducted from the final selling price. Basically, the seller keeps

92.3% of the selling price, after the 7.7% selling fee and $00.25 payment processing fee.

Reverb boasts a simple payout procedure in which they allow the buyer to send the payment to reverb in whatever payment method they prefer, and then the funds are transferred from reverb to the seller's bank account. The payouts are approved 1-2 business days after the item is delivered and can take 1-3 business days to be processed by the seller's bank.

Additionally, there is an option to be paid using PayPal when both the buyer and the seller are PayPal users.

Honest Instruments – This is one of the few other options for musical instrument selling online. Here, things are set up and presented very simply.

The seller has to send in their musical instrument for physical inspection, paying for those fees upfront themselves, and then the site reimburses packing and shipping fees with receipts.

Once the item is received and inspected by honest

instruments, an offer is made. If the seller does not accept the offer, then the site will pack and ship it back to the seller for free.

Payment is made by check in the mail, bank wire, or PayPal.

There is some crucial information that is not readily available, such as more specifics on how listings are created, controlled, maintained. Also, no fees or commissions are to be found.

From the home page, there are two 'buttons' – 'sell music gear' and 'see what you'll get.' Either option walks you through a process to obtain the necessary information to create a price quote.

First, start by selecting the type of instrument, and then you answer a series of questions including brand, model, acoustic or electric, if there is a case, cover or box included, the year the piece came out, serial number, condition on a one to ten scales, the history of the item, any repairs or modifications, then you post pictures of the piece, provide an email address, fill out a form with personal demographics and payment option, and then a representative will contact you with price possibilities.

Where to sell offline:

If you want to sell your musical instrument offline, in person, look up your local avenues, such as music stores, guitar stores, high school, and college music departments, and sometimes places/people who teach music lessons will buy and sell used musical instruments.

Office

It is estimated that a third of Americans are now working from home as a result of the pandemic and the shift to online work.

Even though the outbreak of the pandemic meant that some industries almost completely collapsed, and others are really struggling, there is one type of work that has seen a massive uptick in growth with no signs of letting up. Any type of work that can be done remotely has seen serious growth and is one of the few remaining secure job sources, other than essential needs and services.

With that, many of us are needing to ramp up our home office game.

To be successful either in an actual physical office or working from home, it is very helpful to have the proper gear to be at your most efficient and comfortable.

I badly need a good chair and desk I can fit into my tiny space.

What else makes your ideal office a productive, peaceful environment? Think of those things, and if you have it to let go of, now is a good selling climate to do so.

When I think of office items, all of the big items come to mind first. The desk, chair, and all the crucial electronics.

How about all of the support elements, like calendars, clocks, lighting, footstools, electronic accessories that are not electronic like mousepads, supportive pillows and cushions, keyboard wrist pads, and the list goes on and on.

Then there are the practical implements like staplers,

pens, paper goods, binders, calculators, and anything else that you use to create, store, and organize.

Unless you are selling an entire company's worth of used office items, there are not really any category-specific sites to try.

Instead, utilize all of the sell-almost-anything options such as eBay, Facebook marketplace and groups, craigslist, offerup, letgo, and mercari – or whatever platform you prefer.

As is the case with any other type of item you are selling, don't forget to use these selling tips for best success:

Take great pictures and plenty of them.

Measurements are so very important and will help you find your buyer faster without having to answer the same question over and over.

Find and highlight comparison information for similar items.

When possible, offer the option of selling multiple items as a set. You may take a slight loss in the selling price, but it will mean less hassle because you will deal with fewer buyers.

Be transparent about any defects and flaws.

The usual offline, in-person methods can be used too – garage/yard sales, flea markets, consignment shops, furniture stores, and some pawn shops.

However, if your item is of higher value or serves a specific purpose, selling online will help you target your buying demographic, who is already looking for what you have.

Outdoor and Gardening

Outdoor and gardening as a selling category encompasses a wide variety of items.

You can drive a tractor to plow a field outdoors, but you can also lounge in a hammock outside amid the trees.

Gardening paraphernalia can be as complicated as an entire indoor hydroponic growing system or as simple as hand tools and implements.

Some items are automatically not going to be eligible for resale just because they have already reached their life and will be too worn to try to sell to another person. Those gardening gloves that you love but now have two holes and a permanent smell? Yeah, not selling those.

On the flip side, the riding lawnmower that you used for your old house because you lived on acreage and now live in the suburbs? That is definitely going.

The outdoor and gardening category is not just referring to tools. There is also all of the décor, patio furniture, barbeque pits, and implements, and anything else you can/want to use outside.

In my research and experience, there are no selling platforms or arenas that specifically cater to outdoor and gardening items.

Instead, for these items, you will want to utilize the sell-almost-anything sites like offerup, letgo, craigslist, mercari, Facebook marketplace, and groups and others where a wide variety of products are sold.

The traditional yard/garage sale works great for selling your outdoor and gardening things, and you should explore the flea market route if you are comfortable with that with the whole coronavirus situation. It is, of course, person and situation-specific, but I would say that these types of items are best-sold person to person, in person. Now, you can utilize an online platform such as a Facebook group to find your buyer, but then you must meet them in person. It cuts out the cost of shipping and just seems to be the type of things that are sold more in person.

Use all the same basic tips to sell your items: know your item's value, find the best avenue for you to sell on, take a lot of great pictures, write an eye-catching ad, and when needed – take measurements.

Another thing to note is that some items, especially the high dollar ones, in the outdoor and gardening category, are machinery. This machinery can include things like mowers, weed eaters, lawn edger tools, and other things that have a motor. Make sure that they are running properly before getting started. You never want to go meet someone to sell an item and then are unable to start it. If it is not functioning properly, decide if the necessary repairs will be worth it after you sell the item.

Case in point, my mom and stepdad bought a trailer load full of lawnmowers, all not working, for $250. Because he has skills like that, he was able to get them all up and running for a minimal cost, and they ended up netting over $1,000 (minus my commission fee).

The larger equipment such as riding lawn mowers, tractors, brush hogs, etc., is sometimes a fairly easy and inexpensive fix, and it makes sense to invest in the later return.

Pet

I live in the country, and my dog, Honey, basically roams free and loves it. Please, no judgment, she is very happy and healthy. The reason I start with that personal disclosure is that I have never been a high maintenance pet owner; all of my dogs have been a large breed that lived outside, and the most expensive thing they needed/got was a continuous supply of food.

And to be fair, if you are one of the people who call your pet your fur-baby, no judgment coming from this way either; whatever makes you and them happy.

So – what kind of products can one find for our non-human companions?

Collars, harnesses, nail scissors, toys, leashes, food bowls, pet bedding, crates, small breed coats and shoes, pet carriers, rodent supplies, and this just begins to skim the top of the list.

Sometimes people have a pet that passes away, and they want to get rid of those items. Others, like my friend, review pet products for her blog and regularly amasses a small treasury of items, which she then trades for other items. And, of course, there are plenty of people who get a pet for one of their children, and that situation does not work out, leaving a stockpile of barely used pet supplies.

If you are thinking of selling all of your stuff, as is the purpose of the book, nothing can be overlooked.

I only found one site that specifically bought and sold used pet items:

Netflea - https://www.netflea.com/

Details on the site and how to use it can be found later in the text in the section on all of them on and offline options for selling your stuff.

Since you are so limited in the category-specific sites, you definitely want to make the most of the sell-almost-anything sites that are listed throughout this book and are detailed in the next section – Facebook groups and marketplace, craigslist, offerup, 5miles, letgo, etc.

Your offline options are also the same as the other general items – garage/yard sale, flea market, or using an app to find your buyer and then meet them in person.

Before you go to list your item(s), make sure it is still in great condition and that even the most discerning of used pet product customers will be satisfied.

Also, if it is a specialty item, any sort of food or treats, a new toy, leash, harness, or anything else that could somehow harm a pet, check with one of the sites below to make sure that the item has not been recalled for safety reasons:

American Veterinary Medical Association - https://www.avma.org/news/recalls-alerts

US Food and Drug Administration - https://www.fda.gov/animal-veterinary/safety-health/recalls-withdrawals

Critter Cozy - http://crittercozy.com/CritterCozy-PetFood-Recalls.shtml

School Supplies

Up until I was an adult student, it seemed like, back in the day, that the most expensive school supplies would have been a name-brand backpack, scientific calculator, a band instrument, or some other item that was not necessary for the average student.

That does not seem to be the case now. Well, actually, at this exact moment, in the midst of the pandemic crisis, there are plenty of schools across the country that are only operating virtually. So, parents who once only had to get the usual pens, paper, folders, clothes, and shoes are now having to make sure that their child is equipped for online learning.

Remote education involves, at the minimum, a laptop, some sort of headphones, maybe a webcam, internet connection, and you are lucky if you get away with just those items.

I bring this up right away for two reasons.

One – electronic/technological items will net you the most cash, and you will need to reference that section of the book for tips and details.

Two – After the tech stuff, there is a wide range of items that can be sold. Maybe your child outgrew the need, somehow you ended up with a duplicate, or, if you and your student are fortunate, they just didn't like it, and you ended up replacing it.

So, for anything related to electronics or tech gear – visit the electronic section of this text for those tips and info, and then see the back of the book for details on site-specific information.

The other typical items – pens, binders, paper, pencil holders, calculators, scissors, rulers, backpacks – should be sold on a sell-almost-anything site like good ole Craigslist, Facebook marketplace and groups, eBay, etc.

Because the items listed above are normally not very expensive, try to sell them as a lot.

For those school clothes and shoes that the kids are always outgrowing, see the clothes section of the text.

The purpose of this book is to help you sell all of your stuff, but I do have to include one side note. If the selling of these items doesn't make much difference to you monetarily, please consider donating them to a school in a lower socio-economic area, a children's shelter, a battered women's shelter, or any other community organization that helps to distribute much-needed school supplies to kids who would have a hard time getting them.

Sports Gear and Memorabilia

I will never understand the fascination with sporting and its associated gear and memorabilia. But that's me. I have always been completely indifferent to sports.

That is not the case for many other Americans. There are plenty who pay a pretty penny to go watch their teams in person, invest in their gear, and collect different items associated with their favorite teams.

Because the list of types of sports is so long, there is a very long list of sports gear that can be used for these sports. Now, considering the laws of supply and demand, it makes sense that if you have gear for a sport that is very popular, you will have a large buying demographic. If your chosen sport has a smaller population, you will have a smaller audience and, therefore, will need to take a little more time and put in extra effort to get those items sold.

I had to ask myself – other than bats, balls, and uniforms – what kind of gear could there be for your most popular sports?

Apparently, a lot. Helmets, jockstraps (don't sell these unless they are brand new), mouthguards (same thing), shin pads, ski suits, elbow pads, shoulder pads are some of the items that come up first on the list for individual use.

There is also everything needed to play the sport – rackets, clubs, bats, weights, ropes, nets, shuttlecocks, flags, goals, and the list continues as you delve into all the different kinds of sports.

Before you get ready to decide how you are going to sell your sports gear: make sure that every piece of it is still intact, has minimal wear and tear, is not a used item that touched any intimate part of your body, and ask yourself if you would want to buy that item in the condition you are seeing it in for yourself.

Where to sell used sports equipment online:

Sideline Swap - https://sidelineswap.com/how-it-works

Swap Me Sports - http://www.swapmesports.com/

Gear Trade - https://www.geartrade.com/user/login

And there are the sell-almost-anything sites that can help you get your sports stuff sold – letgo, offerup, Facebook marketplace and groups, mercari, etc.

The sites above allow you to function completely contactless, meaning you send your items in to sell them to the companies.

I did not include any of the local sites because, well, what's local to me could be a thousand miles away for you.

Do an internet search for 'sell used sports equipment near me,' and you are almost guaranteed to find a local sports equipment retailer near you if you live in or near a major city.

The other alternatives for selling your sports gear in person include the typical garage/yard sales, flea markets, and community sales.

For sports equipment, you can include local gyms, schools, training facilities, and anywhere near you where sports are played. Most entities want to pick up gently used sports stuff, so they don't have to pay so much.

Sports memorabilia is another animal.

People who collect or own sports memorabilia enjoy sports to the degree that they collect anything associated with their favorite sport, team, player, etc. These items can become very valuable and have a steady, healthy buying population.

To be considered sports memorabilia, the item simply has to be unique, limited edition, autographed, no longer in production, or any other factor that increases its value.

Some of these items include signed trading CDs, jerseys, photographs, baseball bats and balls, helmets, trophies, football helmets, and many others.

Just like any other valuable item, one of the first things you must do when it comes time to sell it, you need to know its worth, and the best way to do that is with a trained professional – an appraiser.

Use these sites to get your piece appraised as a starting point to getting the most return on your item:

Heritage Auctions - https://www.ha.com/free-appraisals.s?slug=www&ic=WorthFreeAuctionEvaluation

Grey Flannel Auctions - https://greyflannelauctions.com/appraisals.aspx

Lelands Auction Appraisal - https://lelands.com/consign-and-sell

The reason you need an appraisal first is twofold – 1) arming yourself with factual information makes you a confident, informed, and effective seller, and 2) it will either affirm the thought you had that your item(s) were worth big bucks or it will burst your bubble, and you will find out that that card collection is only valuable to you.

Either way, you need to know before you spend any amount of time, effort, or money on selling your sports memorabilia.

When you receive the appraisal, all of the pertinent information you will need, if you didn't already have it, will be included. Things like how the condition is classified, if the item is rare or irreplaceable, the current market, and most often, suggestions on where to sell it.

If your item(s) are even semi-valuable, I would recommend letting a professional site-specific entity handle it for you.

You can skip whatever the associated fees are and go out on your own with the sell-almost-anything sites like offer up, 5miles, letgo, craigslist, etc., but you will probably not get as much money, have to deal with way more hassle, and you don't have a targeted demographic who is searching for your item.

The sites listed below will have detailed information in the next part of the text that includes how it works, details, requirements, etc.:

2nd Markets - http://www.sellsports.us/

Heritage Auctions - https://sports.ha.com/inquire-about-selling.s

Steel City Collectibles - https://www.steelcitycollectibles.com/sell-to-us

Inscriptagraphs - https://inscriptagraphs.com/pages/sell-your-autographs-memorabilia

Kruk Cards - http://www.krukcards.com/

Sidelineswap – All things sports gear related can be bought and sold here. The listed categories of merchandise to be bought and sold includes all sports-related apparel, hockey, golf, skiing, snowboarding, baseball, lacrosse, bikes, alternative hockey, football, softball, tennis, and many other sports-related items. Each sport-specific field has a drop-down menu to show the top subcategory. The mechanics of the site will provide various options and information on how to value your item and then list it.

The process is: create a listing for free using the value guide to price the item appropriately, ship the item (buyers pay for shipping at checkout), and then you get paid.

Of course, as with every online marketplace, it is not quite that simple. Once a listing is created with pictures, details, and price, a buyer can purchase at your listed price or can submit an alternative offer. If both parties come to an agreed-upon price, the buyer pays for the item, sidelineswap sends a prepaid shipping label, and the seller sends the item off.

After the item has been delivered to the buyer for 72 hours and there has been no dispute created by the purchaser, then the funds, minus the selling fees, are transferred to the seller dashboard and can be 'cashed out' using a third party, Payoneer, to transfer the funds from the site to the seller's bank account via ACH transfer.

For the first 1-5 sales, there is a 12% seller fee deducted. Then sales 6 and up incur a 9% seller fee. In addition to these fees, sidelineswap collects a 3% payment processing fee. The minimum seller fee is $1.99, and the maximum is

$100.

In exchange for the fees, the site offers, in return, the following amenities: advertising on major social media sites and many other online and offline avenues where people search for sports gear, prepaid shipping labels, seller protection against chargebacks and fraud, and other helpful services.

GearTrade - The 'gear' bought and sold on this site is focused on outdoor activities like skiing, snowboarding, hiking and camping, climbing, paddling, biking, and other subcategories.

Again, a claim to an easy and simple 3 step process: 1) list your gear by uploading photos, providing a description, 2) ship your gear to the buyer, and then 3) get paid by PayPal, Venmo, or ACH bank transfer.

The commission collected by geartrade is a flat 13% per sale.

There are no fees to list the items, but all shipping and commissions are the seller's responsibility, and the seller should keep this in mind when setting the sale price.

In the information provided by the 'sell your gear' section, there are three payment options listed. However, the terms of use states that payments are made to sellers in the form of a check 9-14 days after the tracking number is received from the seller. The 13% commission is deducted from the sale price, and a check is mailed, according to the terms of use.

It is highly advised with this site and any other online selling platform to thoroughly review all of the available information.

Most claim to be simple and easy with fast payout options, but there are always extra details, processes, policies, etc., that every seller should make themselves familiar with before choosing what platform to use.

Grey Flannel Auctions – This site boasts a staff of experienced sports collectibles specialists with over 30,000 pre-qualified buyers and over $75,000,000 sold in an auction.

There are several options to use with GFA for sports memorabilia items that are valued over $100. You can explore an auction option, consign an item, or sell outright with a competitive cash offer from GFA. There are no specifics listed for any of these avenues. Instead, the seller is directed to fill out an online form, providing personal demographic information, and then send an email with pictures to info@greyflannelauctions.com.

Leland's Auctions – Another high-end sports memorabilia site for the 'serious sports collectors.'

While there are not a lot of specifics provided, the selling options are via auction or consignment.

The seller is encouraged to obtain a free appraisal by filling out the form found on the site with your contact information, information, and/or a description of the item(s), and of course, including photos of the pieces.

Although there is not a lot of details as far as how the process works, fees, commissions, etc., sellers and any other interested parties are encouraged to contact Leland's directly by 732-290-8000 or email:

contact@lelands.com.

For sports memorabilia in the form of collectible cards, try:

Sellsports.us – This site buys these specific items: pre-1970 signed baseballs, pre-1960 sports cards, vintage football memorabilia, baseball memorabilia collections, Michael Jordan rookie cards, vintage basketball memorabilia, Babe Ruth memorabilia, collections, hoarders, estates, or rare singles. For all items, mint or high-grade condition is preferred.

To get in contact with this site and get more information, the interested seller will fill out an online form with personal info and a description of what they have and then follow up with an email with pictures to leads@2ndmarkets.com

Inscriptigraphs - Located in Las Vegas, but 70% of items that are bought to sell online come from out of state or even overseas.

The focus here is on autographed memorabilia for all

types of sports and autographed collectibles from other avenues, including film, TV, and music.

Again, this site is short on specifics such as fees and commissions. They want to see what you have before using either party's time or resources.

Interested sellers are directed to contact 844-474-4633 or send an email with contact information, descriptions, and of course, pictures.

Where to sell offline:

Sports memorabilia is not really something you want to sell with your traditional in-person selling options. Most of your typical garage sale goers are not looking for a thousand-dollar baseball card collection. And if you choose to go the sell-almost-anything site route rather than an auction or selling specific site, be sure to exercise caution and safety.

Tools

As is the case with any item that you are going to sell, the most important question is – what exactly do you have?

When I think of tools, the first thing that comes to mind is hand tools and power tools. You know, the basic things that almost any homeowner and most other individuals in any other dwelling would need to utilize. Things like power drills, maybe some sort of saw, nail gun, etc.

However, if you have a trade or craft or just a specialized hobby, then your idea of tools may be different.

For example, my parents have a huge woodworking shop that houses every type of implement that you could possibly need to create pretty much anything out of wood.

A welder is going to have his own set of specialized tools. As will a jeweler, some crafters, and so on and so on.

The point here is, especially for specialty tools, take the time to do that little bit of research and investigation to find the best avenue to sell your items for top dollar.

For the online option, unless you happen to know of a route-specific to your interest or trade, find a Facebook group or use the marketplace to find other individuals that value those items as much as you do.

For an in-person option, I would suggest something similar. Wherever you originally purchased those items from, see if there is a buyback program, they buy used items, or if they simply can point you in the right direction.

For all tools, you want to utilize the sell-almost-anything sites such as Facebook, letgo, offerup, 5miles, and the others you will see later in the text.

Make sure you include all of the details related to the tool.

Tips for selling tools:

List the make and model number

Be truthful about the condition of the item

Know the purchase date and approximate amount of time that you have been using it

Please, please, please clean it up to the best of your ability

Whether you are selling it to a pawn shop, at a garage sale, or through an online option, you are pretty much guaranteed to get the most when it looks good

Keep all of the tool components together – adapters, chargers, cases, manuals, anything that it originally came with

Have the comparison information ready for what it is worth brand new

There are some brands of tools that will get you top dollar:

Milwaukee

DeWalt

Marita

Bosch

Stihl

Snap-On

And some that will be priced a little lower, just like they were at purchase time:

Rigid

Stanley

Festool

Craftsman

Ryobi

In summary, know what you have, clean it up, weigh your selling options, and decide which way is best for you.

Once last online tip – I have found that including a short video showing the tool in use while powered on can be a great motivator for buyers.

Vehicles

The entire focus of this book is to sell all of your stuff. That includes the '95 Mustang you were hoping to turn into the hot rod of your dreams.

The information included here will all be for selling one private buyer to another.

The first question you have to ask yourself is: what is the reality of selling this vehicle?

Meaning, what needs to be done to get it ready to sell, how much are you willing to invest in getting it sold, and what kind of vehicle is it exactly.

The very first thing I have always done when I have been thinking about buying or selling a vehicle has been to get an up to date monetary figure on the value of the car.

This will help you determine if it is worth it to make any repairs necessary, how much effort you are able/willing to invest in cleaning it, listing it, showing it, etc.

Most car dealers and individuals who regularly sell vehicles will use one of these sites to help get a starting figure on how to value a vehicle –

NADA (National Automobile Dealers Association) – https://www.nada.com/

Edmunds - https://www.edmunds.com/appraisal/

Kelley Blue Book - https://www.kbb.com/whats-my-car-worth/?ico=a

Once you know what the market value for your vehicle is, you then need to assess its condition and what it will take to get it ready to sell.

If you are seeing right away that the vehicle is going to need more than you are able or willing to do to get it to a sellable condition, then you may want to consider selling it as a 'junk car.' No offense intended; I am not saying your car is junk – just a term.

If you are going this route, I would recommend doing a craigslist, Facebook, offerup, or other general selling site search for individuals/entities who buy 'junk' cars in your area. It makes it easier for all parties involved. They pretty much just want to know that you have a title for the vehicle, what condition it is, where you are located, and when you are available to have it picked up.

Alternately, there are some very organized, professional sites that work across the United States to do this same thing. I myself have not tried it, but I can easily assume it is at least a little safer because there is way more of an electronic trail and accreditation to go through.

Try these sites to get a quote on what you can get for your vehicle:

Junk My Car - https://www.junkmycar.com/

Auto Wranglers - https://autowranglers.com/

Car Brain - https://carbrain.com/

Another option for selling your vehicle as a 'junk car' is to contact your local scrap metal or salvage yard, and they will be able to help you. If they themselves do not have a wrecking company that purchases vehicles, they will give you instructions and information on what to do and what to expect.

If your car is not a junk car and you have decided to sell it, you can get the most money for your vehicle by doing these things:

Assess any mechanical damage or issues. The car has to be able to run properly for it to hold its worth. Even if you are not going to fix it before selling it, you want to have this information at the ready so that your buyer can make a fair, informed decision.

Get an inspection and tune-up. A lot of used car buyers are more than a little nervous, possibly in a situation where they need this to happen fast, and this is an overall great selling tool. With a fresh tune-up and inspection, you can claim, with confidence, that this vehicle is legal and roadworthy.

Get a vehicle history report. When selling a car, transparency and honesty are crucial. Do unto others and all that jazz. It shouldn't cost you too much; it lends authenticity to your selling stature and will help net a few more bucks.

A couple of vehicle history report sites to try:

Carfax - https://www.carfax.com/

Vehicle Reports.Net - https://vehiclereports.net/

Vin Audit - https://www.vinaudit.com/

Detail your car. Don't just give it a basic wash. Either get it professionally detailed or take the time to do it yourself. It will make a huge difference throughout the process. Make sure that every nook, cranny, and crevice is clean. Anything that can be opened, moved, or adjusted should be cleaned as if it were new. Address the smell –

make sure the vehicle smells like nothing but cleaning agents and freshness.

Once you get it clean, keep it that way. If you get it detailed and continue to drive it or have it parked, keep it just like the amazing pictures you are going to take.

Take too many pictures. Photograph everything, every angle, the engine, the inside of the trunk, any special features it has. And make sure to highlight anything cosmetically wrong. It will save both you and your buyer time if they can get a clear picture of your vehicle from the plethora of pictures you will provide.

Price competitively. Use the pricing tools mentioned earlier to use as a guide. Then browse other sites where people sell cars to see what it is going for in real life, in your area.

List extensively. Once you have all of the aforementioned steps complete, list your vehicle on as many platforms as possible. Maximum exposure means maximum reach to the maximum audience. If one or more charges for the posting, go ahead and make the investment, the extra attention your vehicle will get will help you get it sold faster and for the price, you are looking for.

Respond promptly. Buyers are going to be actively looking for a vehicle and want quick communication to make their decisions. If you only have certain times that you can communicate, make sure to include that in your listings.

Try these online options for listing your vehicle:

eBay Motors - https://www.ebay.com/b/Auto-Parts-and-Vehicles/6000/bn_1865334

Craigslist - https://houston.craigslist.org/search/cta

Cars.com - https://www.cars.com/

Car Gurus - https://www.cargurus.com/

Auto Trader - https://www.autotrader.com/

To sell as a 'junk' car (see description and details in the previous section):

Peddle - This online marketplace for selling vehicles offers a four-step selling process:

1) 'Tell us about your ride' – the automated system asks the interested seller to provide the year, make, model, the location of the vehicle, details about the condition, and the status of the title.

2) Once all the pertinent details are provided, an instant online offer is established, and the seller can take it or leave it.

3) Upon acceptance of the offer, the date and time are scheduled for a representative to come, verify its condition, and look over the title.

4) Once the vehicle and its condition are verified and the title is confirmed, then the seller is issued a check, the car is loaded up, and everyone parts ways.

Junk Car Zone – This buyer follows a similar format to the one listed above: enter your car information, get an offer, a car buyer specialist comes to your location, and then you get paid, and the vehicle is towed away. The interested seller can start the process by filling out the online form or calling 877-959-9834.

If your vehicle has more life left in it and therefore more value than a 'junk' car, these sites offer vehicle selling options:

Carfax – An all-inclusive used vehicle platform, Carfax offers listing for used cars for sale, Carfax reports, vehicle maintenance tools, suggestions for service shops, currently used car values, and a section to find car news, research, and reviews by entering the vehicle's make model, and year. The Carfax reports are a smart tool to use when selling a vehicle, whether it be through Carfax or anywhere else, because these reports compile a list of information that an interested buyer needs to know. Some of the details included in the reports are major accident history, car ownership lineage, service history, reported damage (hail, structural, and flood), title information, recalls, and much more.

To sell your vehicle with Carfax, you will need to enter in the plate information, state-registered in, current zip code, the VIN, make, model, and year. Then, the car's details, such as trim and options, are entered and confirmed. Finally, choose from local dealers to schedule your car's appraisal to get a real-time cash offer.

CarGurus – For $4.95, you can create a listing to sell your vehicle through CarGurus. With this fee, your listing will be seen by vetted buyers who have been confirmed to be legitimate and valid by providing their ID to a third party, and when a seller completes the sale of the vehicle using CarGurus, they also verify that the buyer has the funds available to complete the transaction.

Listings are active for 30 days and can be extended for free. The 'featured listings' option is $19.99, and this will push your vehicle's listing to the top of the relevant searches. Certainly, an investment to consider if time is of the essence and you want to attract extra attention to your sale.

In short – a) enter the vehicle information to learn its worth, b) gather relevant documents such as title, maintenance history, registration, etc./ c) set your price using the value established in the previous step, write a detailed description that is honest and be sure to highlight any dents, dings, or other issues d) arrange a place and time to meet possible buyers so they can test drive the vehicle e) utilize CarGurus pay so that the funds are filtered from the buyer, through CarGurus to your bank account which helps to remove the possibility of a fraudulent buyer.

CarBuyersUSA – The focus here is on selling your vehicle to this buying entity in a fast, safe, and easy fashion.

The claim is that almost any car in almost any condition in almost any location can be bought by CarBuyersUSA.

Fill out all of the pertinent details on the vehicle you have for sale: year, make, model, VIN, condition, location, title, etc. Send in an email with pictures of the vehicle.

Receive an offer online.

A car buying agent will come to your location once an

appointment is established, or you can choose to meet at a preferred partner location.

Once the vehicle is picked up, the seller is paid on the spot with guaranteed funds.

Cars.com – Use the 'how much is my car worth?' tool to get an up to date valuation on the vehicle using either the license plate or the vehicle specifications, including make, model, year, trim, engine, odometer, and your local zip.

Then you have two options on how to sell your vehicle with cars.com. You can sell to a dealer to sell your car quickly using the same information needed to find the value of the car. Interested parties will then contact you with offers.

The second option is to sell it yourself to an independent buyer. This option may take more time and effort but will almost always result in getting more money for your vehicle. For $4.95, the basic package allows a seller to upload up to 10 photos, running the listing for 30 days, and free renewals after the initial 30 days.

In summary, cars.com offers multiple selling options, tips on how to sell your vehicle fast, and other tools on the site to help the buyer and seller make informed and fair decisions.

AutoTrader- With an excellent, long time reputation for facilitating vehicle buying and selling, this site claims to be the only website with "more than 3 million vehicle listings from over 40,000 dealers, and 250,000 private owners".

With this type of exposure to interested buyers, sellers can expect to pay a little more, but this added expense should help you find a reasonable price from a real buyer in an expeditious manner.

To create a listing, there are three package options: basic - $25.00 includes 3 photos, an ad on KBB with upgrade options; featured - $50.00 includes 20 photos, an ad on KBB and upgrade options; premium - $90.00 includes 30 photos, and add on KBB, and three upgrade options come as part of the package – a vehicle history report, supercharger feature that boosts your listing's exposure, and a spotlight amenity to bring you more buyers faster.

All three of the listing options will run for 30 days and then can be renewed for free for another 30 days.

If you do not want to go through the time and efforts necessary to create a listing and find the right buyer, there is another option.

The Kelley Blue Book Instant Cash Offer uses your vehicle's specific features and conditions to create an offer that is valid for 7 days, then you take the vehicle to a participating dealer, and finally, the vehicle is sold there for cash or used as a trade-in credit.

This option is free to use and can be the fastest option with the least amount of effort, but that, of course, means that the cash price received or the trade-in valuation will be lower than selling from one independent party to another.

Be sure to also use the sell-almost-anything sites because those listings are cheap or free and will help you to reach the widest audience possible.

Video Games

Just like with all other technology, there are three essential things to remember when selling video games.

Firstly – sell early. Video games lose their value as new versions are released, new game systems come out, and technology continues to update. If you are thinking of selling any of your gaming systems, games, and components, don't sit on it, they depreciate quickly.

Second – take care of the game(s) and all that goes along with it. Clean them up, store them properly, and hold on to everything that it originally came with. Anything that has a 'like new' quality will sell faster and for much more.

Lastly – shop around. The more platforms you use to sell your items, the better your chances of fetching the price that you are looking for. Compare different sites' fees, processes, and shipping costs before making a final decision.

Of course, you can utilize the sell-almost-anything sites, but your chances of achieving the sale that you are looking for are higher when you use sites that specialize in your item.

Try these sites for your gaming items:

eStarland - https://www.estarland.com/

Trade4Cash - http://www.trade4cash.com/

Gameflip - https://gameflip.com/

Game Stop - https://www.gamestop.com/trade/

Decluttr - https://www.decluttr.com/

If you have vintage video games, try these sites:

The Old School Game Vault - https://theoldschoolgamevault.com/

DK Oldies - https://www.dkoldies.com/sell-your-games/

There is one more option to consider when thinking about selling anything related to games. I was surprised to learn that you can sell your video game player account. Basically, whatever stature or rank you have built up for yourself has value, and these sites will help you sell it:

Player Auctions - https://www.playerauctions.com/sell-other-games-account/

Player Up - https://www.playerup.com/

GamerMarkt - https://www.gamermarkt.com/en

eStarland - This gaming platform focuses on all kinds of games, accessories, and systems and claims to accept more than any of the other competitors.

There are three ways to get value from your gaming component. eStarland calls them trade-in options:

Instant trade-ins are basically just like the name implies.

You add the item(s) you want to trade-in to your shopping cart, then add the purchases you wish to make to the same cart, and while your new purchase is on the way, prepare and mail your item in to finalize the trade.

The selling point for this option is that it is the most convenient, you are able to trade one item for another with no waiting, but your credit card will be authorized until your trade-in is received and the process is complete.

Standard trade-ins – This method means there is no exchange of items; you are simply adding the trade-in item(s) to the cart, checkout the item(s), and then ship those items in.

The most traditional trade-in option and the option that offers the most value. Credits are issued only after the trade-in item is received, and eStarland will help with the shipping and packaging supplies reimbursement after the trade-in process has been completed.

Sell your games is the only option to get actual cash. Almost the same procedure – add your trade-ins to the shopping cart, ship the items in by the due date, and once the confirmation email is received from the site, you can cash out from your account.

The upside to this option is that its trade-in value is enumerated in monetary form.

The downside is that the value of the trade-in is 70% of the item(s) value.

Payment options are check payment by mail in 4-7 business days, amazon gift card in 2-7 business days, or PayPal payment in 2-7 business days.

Gameflip – There are several ways to make money on this gaming site. There are competitions that offer cash rewards, in-game items can be bought and sold, gaming systems and their components, gift cards, and the more tab include the options of selling movies, gigs, accessories, and collectibles.

Not only can you sell your gaming items, but you can also sell achievements from games such as in-game items and skins, use gaming skills to coach and teach others, or pick up a gig using your creative skills.

Whatever you are selling with this site, the process is the same: a) create an account for free, b) list your item as detailed and accurate as possible with a reasonable price that is comparable to what others are selling for, c) seller is notified when an item sells and then guided through the transaction process, d) sales are deposited into the 'wallet' feature once the buyer has received the item and completes the transaction by assigning a rating to the item received. Once this process is complete, the monies can be transferred from the wallet to your bank or payment account at any time.

Gameflip takes an 8% commission plus a 2% digital fee when applicable off of the listing price.

There are lots of options, details, and other pertinent information that should be carefully reviewed.

The Old School Game Vault – specializes in the buying and selling of older gaming units, including Nintendo, Sony PlayStation, Xbox consoles, and retro gaming consoles and games.

To sell your old school gaming components, you locate the item(s) you wish to sell, click the 'sell it' button, fill up the shopping cart until there is at least a $15 minimum. Shipping labels are provided for orders above $75, orders between $75-100 will have a $10 fee deducted for shipping costs, and all orders over $100 get a free shipping label.

Then, you send in an email to let the site know that your items are on the way. Once received, tested, and inspected, the payment is issued via the method you choose within 24-96 hours of receipt of your items.

Payout methods are amazon gift cards sent to your email address, PayPal payments that are almost instantly available, or business checks sent in the mail that generally arrive in 1-5 business days.

PlayerAuctions – Although both virtual and physical products can be sold with this platform, there is a heavy emphasis on the selling of virtual items. The virtual goods that can be sold include gold, accounts, items, skins, boosting services, leveled accounts, and other achievements that a player has earned and is now ready to sell to another gamer.

To start the selling process, the seller will need to register and then list what they have to sell. Once a product is purchased, an email notification will be sent. Payments will be made to the seller's Skrill, Payoneer, or bank account.

It is free to register and list your gaming items, and fees are only assessed when a sale is made.

The fees are dependent on what the item or service is and vary from 9.99% + $00.99 to 14.99% + $00.99. There are also disbursement fees depending on how you choose to be paid out.

Vintage Items

The difference between vintage and antique is simply age. An item can be considered a vintage item if it is between 20-100 years old, whereas an antique item is normally classified as an antique when it hits that 100-year mark.

After you determine what age category your item belongs in, vintage or antique, you can start to think about how and where to sell your item(s).

A lot of the selling options for antiques and vintage items will overlap simply because these are not just 'used' items that are being sold. Their value comes from the timeframe they were first created, their rarity, and the current demand for the item.

Just because your item can technically be considered vintage does not necessarily guarantee that it has the value you are looking for. There are plenty of items that are twenty-plus years old that should only be sold at a garage sale because they are not worth the time it would take to sell them any other way.

However, see if what you have falls into the list below:

Vintage toys – Star Wars, Polly Pocket, early Spiderman, and Batman and these items are especially valuable when in their original packaging and in mint condition

Pyrex – Almost every home that has at least one hand-me-down has a piece of Pyrex. Depending on the condition, the edition, the colors, if it is a full set, and the collectability, your piece of glass may be worth a pretty penny.

Vintage comics that inspired movies – Since the release of the movie Black Panther, all of the original comics associated with it have skyrocketed in value.

Advertising signs – Check out that old Pabst sign your aunt, who owned a bar for twenty years, gave you. You might be surprised to find out how much you can get for it.

Boy Scout memorabilia – I can see it. It's an organization steeped in tradition, so it makes sense that there is a demographic interested in all things related to their group.

Pokémon cards – Complete sets and ultra-rare cards will, of course, bring in the most cash.

American Girl Dolls – These dolls from the mid-1980s still have a collector following, and if yours is in good condition, it may net you a nice chunk of change.

Typewriters – Just because it is 'old' doesn't mean it will sell. But if it is in good condition and it works properly, there are plenty of people who will pay for your old typewriting machine.

If you don't have anything on this list, never to fear – this is just a small list of ideas. If what you have is in good condition, do a quick google search and see if there are buyers out there actively searching for it.

Where to sell your vintage items:

Etsy - https://www.etsy.com/

Bonanza - https://www.bonanza.com/

Ruby Lane - https://www.rubylane.com/

Art Fire - https://www.artfire.com/

eBid - https://www.ebid.net/us/

Some other, in-person options for selling your vintage items include:

Consignment stores

Garage/yard sales

Pawnshops

Antique stores

Auction houses

And, of course, you can always utilize the sell-almost-anything sites. Just be very clear and specific that you are aware that this is a vintage item, what you expect for it, and have your research ready to back up your price.

Chapter 11: How to Throw a Great Garage Sale

One of the classic ways to get rid of your stuff is to hold a yard sale (or garage sale). Here are the steps for making yours as successful as possible.

1. Check the rules in your locality. Some Homeowner's Associations do not permit yard sales due to increased traffic in the neighborhood. Also, check your city ordinances for posting signs to advertise your yard sale.

Rules will vary by jurisdiction.

2. Pick a date and time. I have had the best experience running my sale on Friday and Saturday from 7am to noon. You'd be surprised at the early birds who will swarm your sale as soon as it opens to snag the best deals.

3. Organize and price your stuff. The advice varies on this, but I have found it best to buy those little round price tag stickers and price your items. Leave a little haggle room and price items fairly. Too high, and the buyer may be turned off from the sale. Too low, and you'll cheat yourself out of fair money.

4. Have cash for change, including coins.

5. Advertise! Post signs first thing that morning at major intersections that lead to your neighborhood. Use bright colors, with large font and arrows with your address. If you can, buy a post in the classified ads section of your local newspaper. Post your sale in locally-based Facebook groups that allow advertising.

6. Notify your neighbors. You may, as a courtesy, consider telling your immediate neighbors when you're holding a yard sale. They may expect increased traffic and more cars parked on the street for that day. I have also found that my immediate neighbors were sometimes my best customers!

7. Organize your items and display them pleasingly. Keep like items grouped together—place items on tables as you can to keep them off the ground. Keep the most valuable items closest to you so you can keep an eye on them.

8. Offer your customers a shopping bag. You know we all have some plastic or paper grocery bags lying around. Keep these for the sales day for your customers as a courtesy.

9. Keep an eye on your sale. Yes, people can shoplift your yard sale items.

10. Consider making the last hours of your sale a half-off special. You really don't want this stuff back, so consider selling at a clearance price.

11. Consider sales bundles, such as "buy 2, get 1 free," especially with children's toys and clothing.

12. Consider holding paid for items for later pick up. Make a plan with the buyer if they need to come back later to retrieve the items.

With these simple tips, your yard sale should go very well.

Conclusion

Thank you for reading my book all the way to the end. I hope you have learned something about the importance of decluttering, not only for the financial value but also for the emotional value.

As I have finished this book, the threat of the global pandemic has not lessened. I have managed to sell much of the stuff that was in my grandmother's RV and have put some money in my emergency fund from the sales.

I hope that you have learned how to let go of your old stuff and how not to accumulate more needless stuff in the future. I don't advocate a necessarily "minimalist" lifestyle, but I think there is beauty in the simple things. At the end, who could argue with making money off of things that are otherwise just sitting around?

If you would be so kind, I would really appreciate it if you would leave a review online where you purchased this book. Online reviews can help my book reach a wider audience. Thank you in advance!

Printed in Great Britain
by Amazon